MODERN PROPAGANDA

J.M. DEL HAGEN

Modern Propaganda
[mod-ern] [prop-uh-gan-duh]

Noun
The art of influencing society, individuals, and businesses through digital communication. Also includes the interpretation and manipulation of data analytics and patterns to influence behavior.

CONTENTS

Forward

In a world that is fake, how do you tell what is real?

In a world that actually prefers the fake over the real, how do you win?

It is human nature to gravitate towards manufactured realities. The Internet is ideally suited to cater to these desires and has, unlike any other force, heralded in the age of Modern Propaganda.

The simple truth is Modern Propaganda is as much about giving people what they want, as it is about steering and influencing what they believe in. Before reading this book, it is important to understand that this book can be manipulative in nature. I intentionally wrote from the perspective of how to sway sectors of society through digital means.

On the Internet, much of the noise and political outrage we see when a topic is brought to the forefront of our perception is nothing more than provoked emotional feeling, manufactured for consumption. To that extent, I put forth that it is better to understand the machinery that drives one's perception of reality, than it is to ignore it.

My intention is that this book will enable you to not only learn some more advanced propaganda techniques but to more easily understand and identify when you are being manipulated.

Ultimately, each of us casts our own shadow on reality in search of our own truth.

J.M. del Hagen

1
BUILDING REALITY

"A person would rather hear a lie than hear the truth.
Again, a person would rather hear a lie than hear the truth".
- J.M. del Hagen

If you have been in the Internet tech industry long enough you will understand what I mean by this statement. If you have not been in the tech industry, you may have witnessed this phenomenon as well. However, I have come to the conclusion that the insistence by individuals that you lie to them is most pervasive in things driven by data.

Before reading this book further, you should understand this fundamental concept. To be clear, this is **NOT** to say you **should** lie, however, just that some would **rather** that you lie to them. In fact, you should avoid lying whenever possible, regardless of whether the person insists you lie to them.

Along these same lines and therefore, by extension;

It is easier for you to tell a lie than tell the truth.

And to be sure, for many who work in the digital sector of society, those who do lie will have a strategic advantage **temporarily** over those who do not. Furthermore, by the time a person goes through two or three liars and finally works with a trustworthy consultant, they are so tainted by the liars that they think you're the liar. The situation is far too common in the industry.

Truth be told, it is not the individual's fault. They don't really **want** you to lie to them, they simply want what they know as their version of reality to be true. They are bombarded daily with fake Twitter accounts who enrage or delight them, media who feeds them distorted reality, and yes, propagandists who capitalize on them.

Let us not forget the unscrupulous salespeople desperate to make a living on the Internet, or simply displaced workers with little or no knowledge of how technology or Internet marketing works, who have become enablers and have flooded into the digital spaces.

This is further compounded by the sheer volume of information and data on the Internet, the size of which is so astronomical, business owners have a hard time grasping the reality of the digital world they wish to enter. The digital world is ripe for disruption or exploitation of unsuspecting individuals.

To gain context, look closely at the following stats. There are 510 million live, active websites on the Internet and by the time you read this there will be millions more. These websites produce an astounding, 30,000,000,000,000 indexed web pages. The Google Knowledge Graph Tool estimates that Google, Amazon, Microsoft and Facebook store at least 1,200 petabytes of data between them.

Inside the world of social media, it is estimated there are 2.4 MILLION FACEBOOK POSTS PER MINUTE and 3.5 BILLION Facebook messages posted daily. On Twitter, there are 40 MILLION tweets shared each day, and let us not forget e-mail and spam which is estimated to produce 294 BILLION emails every day. And now for the kicker, people trying to sort through this information perform 6 BILLION Google searches each day.

The sheer volume of information is enough to baffle even the most brilliant among us. To cope with these numbers, the average user personalizes the Internet experience to be about "me". While service providers go through great efforts to mimic a personalized experience, this perception is false. In the end, each person, each search, is part of a modern machine. This machinery is composed of bits and bytes, scripts, servers, browsers and operating systems with the Internet as a backbone, all designed to give the user a false perception of reality.

Don't believe me? It is thought that Google's own code base, the lines of programming to make the Google software, spans 2 billion lines. An average of 25,000 software engineers can add to and work on Google at the same time. That is more people than many towns in the United States.

A person is helpless when presented with the massive volume of data. They have no choice but to use a preconceived notion of truth to navigate these waters, in the hope of getting actionable intelligence, on which to act.

No choice? Well, perhaps, that is not quite accurate. Of course, individuals have a choice. They can choose to bury their heads in the digital sands and ignore the manipulation that is going on around them. Or they can act to understand that influencing and interpreting data is key to building their own world. Otherwise, they risk being subjected to the whims of those who lead them.

Should you feel bad for the individuals who are being manipulated daily? No. If you attempt to educate them, they will scorn you, belittle and devour you, until you accept that what they believe is true. An individual must understand the machinery of Modern Propaganda on their own accord and in their own time.

Is Modern Propaganda New?
Not really. It is the information age's answer to propaganda that has existed for years. Then, as with now, you need smart-thinking people to carry out the mission of creating the propaganda.

A Changing Wind. What Changed?
For the past 100 years, the art of influencing the masses was driven by propagandists that specialized in triggering the desire to consume. While driving the consumption of products is still important in the digital landscape; power, politics, and social power have come to the forefront. The Internet can level the playing field, making the largest competitors vulnerable to attack. No longer are you subject to the gateway of network television and nightly TV news. You simply must possess the technical prowess and resources to work online.

Along those lines, today's agencies have come to the realization that they are as much immersed in technology as creativity. For years, ad agencies resisted this truth and treated Internet data architects as nothing more than common workers. As demonstrated by events like SxSW and The Cannes Lions International Festival of Creativity, agencies realized that this philosophy of not accepting the digital reality around them has failed. As technology empires were built without them, the vast wealth they accumulated in traditional media, like TV advertising, began to erode. To some, technology was a welcome savior, to others, it meant death. Now, many scramble to catch up as advertising distribution is controlled by technology players globally.

Internet and technology executives were also guilty of the same folly as the agencies. They produced incredibly sophisticated technological achievements with little to no style which made consumer reaction lackluster at best. They treated marketing agencies, and the ability to influence behavior, as beneath them or immoral, resulting in countless lost opportunities.

> *Individuals that are able to blend the two worlds of data and artistry are an essential element of Modern Propaganda.*

Thoughts On the Mind

To the uninitiated, the mind is like a concrete barrier. To the skilled practitioner of Modern Propaganda, it is a panacea of triggers and puzzle pieces waiting to be manipulated with precision data. When emotion is removed from thought, creating Modern Propaganda strategies becomes a relatively simple endeavor. This is not to say one should be emotionless; just that removing emotion from the equation can lead to more effective decision making.

Equally at play is direct data manipulation. When done correctly, it is possible to affect the outcomes of millions of individuals, even if very slightly. Many take issue with the direct data manipulation method. However, its value cannot be understated and should be considered at all times. To this point, I give you the group 4Chan, whose members are widely considered to be some of the best propagandists in the world. Their methods range from basic to inhumane, yet the results are undeniable. And while some of the tactics they have taken can be considered cruel and very distasteful. To that extent I say:

"Don't Shy From Them, Hire Them."

We must keep a stable of talent that is, not only technically sophisticated, but, able to see propaganda for what it is. Furthermore, they must be able and willing to do unsavory acts when needed for the cause. Those individuals who are soft will fail, those who are strong will endure, yet those who possess the intelligence to manipulate the mind will ultimately win.

To the question, "Is propaganda manipulation ethical?", I say, "Who cares." One need only go into Twitter for brief periods of time to see college professors pushing political agendas, media outlet skewing news, and the masses following in bliss. Furthermore, the vast majority of the loud voices not only lack the common sense needed for sound decision making, they also seek to rule you. Only a fool would allow someone with inferior intellect to dictate terms to live under. Therefore, is propaganda ethical? Yes. It is ethical and, in fact, necessary, to combat the deluge of inferior logic, lies, and control in today's world.

Furthermore, manipulation allows you to keep control of the message and ensure it will get out. Without leveraging this tactic, one must have a superior idea or fame which is rare and unpredictable at best.

2
SPYING AND INTELLIGENCE GATHERING

Spying is so common on the Internet that anyone who trusts that their data is fully secure is a fool.

Your enemy is strategic in nature and will use every tool in their arsenal to understand the 'how and why' of what you are doing. They will scan you, slam you, attack you, all in an effort to gain an advantage. If you are in a competitive vertical market the situation is far worse.

Therefore, your enemy must be treated with respect and contempt. Everyone in your organization must have the same contempt and focus on destroying the enemy. They must be instilled with the belief that their livelihood depends on beating the enemy; *for it does*. They must be constantly vigilant that the enemy may be attacking you; *for they are*. The team must constantly leapfrog past the enemy and strategically outthink them to survive. In the end, the most powerful diatribe in the world is not going to have an effect, unless your team can do the work needed to gather intelligence on your enemy.

> ### *In Modern Propaganda,*
> ### *your competitors are enemy number one.*

Your Visibility Into a Competitor is Limited
I will now discuss some of the common tools and techniques used for spying on the enemy. However, unless you are able to somehow access the internal analytics of the company you are spying on, you will never have a full view into all of their digital positions.

Tools are just that, tools. They give you a limited view into a situation. As long as you understand these rules, it is incredibly useful to understand a competitor's digital footprint. Some of my favorite tools for spying include: MajesticSEO, SEMrush and aHrefs.

Natural Organic Search
Perhaps one of the most published and sought after views into a competitor is how well they search in Google and other search engines. This is called organic search.

However, the simplistic days of looking at single key terms to see how well they rank (show up on page one of Google) are over. Search providers now have root terms, channels, and thousands of variations of terms associated with a single searched root keyword. For example, you could type the word 'Pizza' (Root) or 'Locate a Pizza Place' (Variation).

Some recent estimates suggest that as many as 20% of all searches are new every month. I tell you this only for the fact that you may well spy on a competitor who has what you think are great *key term search ranks* only to find they don't actually convert that well, so use caution. We have a saying in the industry, *ranks do not equal conversion*.

> ### *Ranks do not equal conversion.*

In other words, because you *guess* that a search term is what consumers are looking for does not mean it is true. The other issue is just because a search provider reports that a single keyword has a number of searches each month does not mean it's true, which I will cover in more detail later.

Right now you may be wondering, what does this have to do with Modern Propaganda? Well, everything. A website is a hub that, when setup properly, acts as a distribution and dissemination point of your data to the Internet at large.

When doing organic search research, you will want to look to look at five factors:

- High Volume Search Keywords
- What New Competitors Are Using These Search Keywords
- Changes in Search Positions Over Time
- Landing Pages Competitors Are Using to Achieve These Search Keywords
- Estimated Cost of These Keywords (*If You Need to Buy Search Exposure for The Keywords*)

Organic Footprint

Once you have an idea about the organic search landscape of your competitor, it is time to understand how they did this. The most common place to start is the *link profile*. A *link profile* is really a breakdown of who and what is linking to the competitor's website. Be advised, many stray paths have been taken by those who follow this profile blindly. You do not necessarily want to copy your competitor's digital footprint strategy. You need to take into account changes that have occurred to search algorithms over time. The digital world is an ever moving river and you must know where exactly on the river you are putting your tube in the water, or risk being smashed against the rocks.

With that caveat, the five factors you will look at are:

- **Backlinks**: Indicates the website and page your competitor is getting a link from.
  Example: Link from New York Times
  Source URL: http://www.newyorktimes.com
  Enemy URL: http://www.enemy.com
- **Anchors:** Indicates the type of link (Follow, NoFollow) and keywords if any that were used to link to a competitor's website.
- **Unique Websites:** This is a list of websites that link to your competitors.
- **IP Address**: Unique servers linking to the competitor.
- **Indexed Pages:** Indicates the number of pages that are indexed in the search engines.

Search Marketing Maps Versus TV DMA Maps

In the world of paid TV advertising, Nielsen ratings are the gold standard for tracking the effectiveness of TV reach. To mark out areas of the country, they use something called DMA's (Designated Market Areas).

While it is possible in Google to buy Pay-Per-Click by DMA, this targeting is far from accurate on the Internet. The reason is that the Internet traditionally works most effectively in small radiuses around a target.

I have seen many traditional ad agencies attempt to force their staff to use the outdated DMA model, resulting in poor pricing and business models; *beware of this trap*.

Therefore, when spying on an enemy's advertising online, it is important to understand how the paid ads truly work and are displayed on the Internet, in order to have a proper sense of just how your competitor's ads are being viewed.

To illustrate the point, I have created two maps which are available on the website. One is called a DMA - Designated Market Areas map, the other is an ISM - Internet Search Map.

I Spy

Now that you have a basic understanding, it's time to spy.

When doing paid ad research, investigate a competitor's buying habits:

- **Types of ads** (PPC, Video, Display Advertising (*Including Re-Targeting*), Instream App / Social, and Product Buy Now Ad's)
- **Placement of the Ads**
- **Copy or Media Type of Ads**
- **Ad History and Estimated Spending**
- **Ad Landing Pages**
- **Other Competitors**

Some of the aspects you will look for are: the keywords competitors have in common, the amount of traffic they receive, branded versus non-branded traffic and reputation. Once you gather this intelligence, you can effectively use it to wage a paid media campaign. However, I caution you, the Internet is always evolving and taking technological leaps forward, therefore, it is best to learn and innovate with new strategies when it comes to paid digital media.

Advertising Fraud

Ahh, you thought I would simply outline some technical information on how to spy on your competitors? Well, paid digital media like all things on the Internet is rampant with fraud. This fraud adds to the high cost of paid ads. While many providers have helped curb the once systemic issue, fraud is big business.

Click Fraud

The most common form of fraud is local click fraud. Very simply, a local competitor sees your ad running and starts clicking on it, or asking their associates to do the same. With some highly competitive pay per click ads costing upwards of a few hundred dollars, you can rather quickly ring up a hefty bill for an unsuspecting target.

The next form of click fraud is a bit more calculated. In this model, 3rd party *publishers* make an advertising deal with one of the major search *advertising networks*. The *publisher's* site looks legitimate enough, and in fact, they may even have real users using their site. However, amongst the real users are plants whose job it is to click on the ad's running on the publisher's website. Every time an ad is clicked the publisher gets a piece of the action. In many cases, they will try to use overseas staff with local proxies to do this.

Malware Hijacking

Another method of publisher fraud is Malware hijacking. In this method, a virus software writer will do a deal with a number of publishers or advertising aggregators to fleece unsuspecting businesses out of their cash. The virus software writer gets as many web browsers or machines infected as possible. The virus then serves ads and clicks on behalf of the user. Because the infected machines are, in fact, real users it is incredibly difficult to detect.

Lead Scraping

Lead scraping is another method we see commonly used. This is where a group will set up a website to sell business leads to another business. These leads can be legal, dental, plastic surgery, etc. To accomplish this, the software programmer will write a type of virus or malware that infects as many web browsers as possible. However, instead of clicking on ads to generate revenue, the virus scans the website a real user is viewing, interprets that copy, and puts a fake contact form that matches the material on the website. For example, a user might be looking for a local dentist and viewing their local website of www.dentist.com. A fake contact form will appear that actually looks like the dentist asking you to contact them. The contact from is never sent, instead the lead is harvested by the virus and sent to a high bidder, which is normally a competitive business. For this scam to work, it takes both a local business willing to buy the harvested leads and a very sophisticated malware software writer. This is an extraordinarily profitable business model with plenty of local businesses willing to buy.

Buying Leads
When it comes to the matter of buying leads on the Internet, I say either the lead source is legitimate, or it is not. In the case where it is legitimate, you can expect the lead provider to be expensive and sell to multiple parties. In the case where the provider is not legitimate, you may have great success, or be taken advantage of, in which case, you have no recourse.

Why DMA's Have Changed to SMA's (Search Market Areas)
So, here is where the web is not only interesting but disruptive. My team and I used to joke that you could cut off Internet access to the entire East Coast by chopping this ONE fiber optic cable that ran between Boston and New York. No, I am not going to tell you where the cable is. But all joking aside, it is relevant to our discussion. In the early days of the web, there was a race to provide bandwidth. Companies like RCN, Verizon, AT&T, UUNET and Sprint all raced up and down the East and West coasts of the United States installing a miracle material called *fiber optic cable*.

In many cases, these were not hundreds of small cables but **one** giant backbone fiber optic cable that carried massive amounts of data. They were installing what is called the *backbone of the Internet*. This backbone gets to the reason why the Internet works by radius, instead of TV DMA.

Geo location of search relied strictly on IP based networks, which in turn relied on where the phone and fiber optic carriers placed their cables in the ground. The result was that the user would get an IP address that was far from their location. Search results and advertising would read that IP and display ads from that far away location. For example, you could be in city A and pulling results from city B, which is 30 miles away from you and so on.

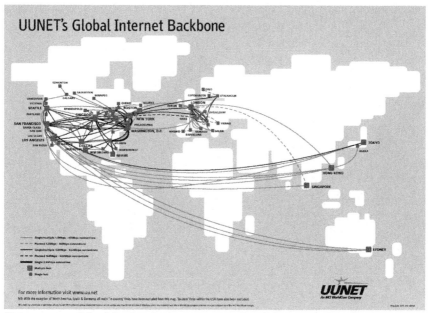

This was not ideal for business owners who did not service distant clients and it was not ideal for producing relevant consumer search results. Many of these issues have been solved with the Geo Location Targeting through the use of Mobile Devices. However, to this day, geo located search results still have issues.

Now, when it comes to the issue of selling advertising on the Internet, you can either chose to disclose this information or not. In the case where you choose to disclose this information, you will likely confuse the business owner and complicate the sale. In the case where you choose not to disclose this information you simplify the sale, and have control of the spending of the client. In truth, provided you are a legitimate consultant, I say it is better to be in perception. As a result, not only do you retain the power, but you keep the client from doing harm to themselves. In the case where your intent is not so pure, then it does not matter what you disclose anyway.

3
SOCIAL MEDIA SWARMS

It is estimated that the group called ISIS (Islamic State in Iraq and Syria) had over 90,000 Twitter accounts that it used to recruit fighters to its global war. While fairly simplistic in nature, the group is relevant in that it is using modern, decentralized communication to establish battlefield and information dominance. The decentralization of communication messages is difficult to control, yet, can be easy to counter-act with the right strategy.

To start with, the vast majority of these users are fake and are termed *Social Media Swarms*.

Unfortunately, government agencies, likely due to bureaucratic central control, find this challenging at best. However, if deployed correctly, a government can marshal considerable resources to wage a formidable counter attack.

As the online newspaper, "The Guardian", so eloquently summed up in a piece written by Patrick Kingsley, *"Who is behind Isis' terrifying online propaganda operation? "*

> *"The extremist jihadist group leading the insurgency against the Iraqi government is using apps, social media and even a feature-length movie to intimidate enemies, recruit new followers and spread its message. And its rivals – including foreign governments – are struggling to keep up." ***
>
> *http://www.theguardian.com/world/2014/jun/23/who-behind-isis-propaganda-operation-iraq

Mr. Kingsley is absolutely correct, and while I have used the opening lines of this chapter to discuss the global warfare propaganda, the same methods of *social media swarming* can also be applied to spreading messages for international NGO's, politicians, corporations and your clients.

Perhaps more frightening than the Modern Propaganda aspect, is that the same theories that have created Modern Propaganda have been effectively applied by groups like ISIS in creating a new, modern, decentralized armies which I will cover in more detail later on in this book. Fortunately, most of us are not seeking to enslave mankind into some apocalyptic vision.

Flocking or Blocking? That is the Question
To deploy your own social media swarm, I like to start with something I call *flocking technology*. The name is trite but the concept can be used to do everything from promoting new brands, to launching new products and more. The system can be further refined for use in establishing global social media networks.

Let's take a case where you want to counteract a group that is using Twitter, or a similar micro blogging service, to bash a particular political party. While it is true that grander concepts like the user's preconceived notion about the political party in question play a key factor with regards to influence, technology and the personal interaction it brings to the individual. This is the hook which compels action.

Flocking technology creates a social media storm by magnifying a single user account into many. Like a giant megaphone, this technology also has the advantage of creating a bandwagon effect which accumulates real, non-paid, non-computer generated users to your flock.

The goal is to turn your controlled flock of 'fake bots' into a social media swarm where real users perpetuate the message you're trying to convey. To do this we need to follow some basic steps. It is also important to keep in mind that a flock is an asset that should be built over years, not months, if you wish it to have any long term value.

Stage 1 of Flocking: Seeding

To demonstrate a real world example, let's take some of the recent political campaigns or what some would call old fashioned social media mudslinging. We will first create a pretend group called, United For Change, along with a Twitter hashtag #UnitedForChange which is started by a *seed user* on Twitter. A seed user is an actual, real user or aged account that has over 1,000 real followers of which very few are robots.

Within the primary seed's Twitter followers, we are going to add 20 new fake accounts and use an off the shelf software package like Hootsuite to manage our 20 fake accounts in order to create around 475 users each. Now, within the 20 new accounts we are going to add around 100 accounts with up to 250 users. Last, we will buy or create robots and establish 1,000 additional disposable Twitter accounts.

Does this sound exponential? It is.

To review we now have: 1 x (Primary Seed User) + 20 x (Secondary Seed Users) + 100 x (Tertiary Seed Users) + 1,000 x (Disposable Accounts). It is also important to note that except for the 1,000 disposable accounts, these users should have fake photos added to their accounts to give the feeling of a genuine person. This is your seed flock.

Stage 2 of Flocking: Scripting

While there are many social media tools which are great for building up your primary seed flock, they are not so great at managing your message on a global scale. This requires building out custom software or modifying off the shelf software to fit your needs. Your internal team should be able to readily build this out for you. I call this component a *flock controller*.

The basic premise of our *flock controller* is to create the illusion of mass outrage or the ground swell of a message. Therefore, to start, we need an interface where we can load our master user /admin. The admin will need to load multiple tiers of users.

Historic diagram of a flock controller:

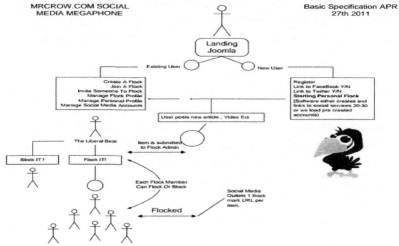

Once your scripts are built, you will begin to load the individual Twitter accounts with seed content. Each subsequent account will re-tweet the primary and so on. Keep in mind that your coders should use a variable, re-tweeting, algorithmic pattern so they appear random, otherwise, you risk being detected or even banned by the Twitter admin services.

When architected properly, your *flock controller* will give the audience the illusion of a mass outrage over a subject matter, which will in turn incentivize real users to join your flock. Once you get a critical mass of real users, a viral effect comes naturally. Furthermore, media and journalists will be enticed to join the social media feeding frenzy. Keep in mind it is best to start these flocks around issues that have some truth to them, this way the credibility of the subject matter withstands scrutiny and opposition that will surely follow.

Thoughts on Fake Activism

While the current trend of paying activists to protest and slander opponents has shown to be very effective I do question whether the more educated will catch on to the tactics or will have noise burn out. However, until the burn out occurs, I say use this tactic to its fullest. Ideally, you can find a real protest that has gone viral on Twitter and has an existing, trending #hashtag. Once identified, use your non-profit arm to cover their expenses and spread the protest, preferably to Universities, as the students tend to be naive of the manipulation and like to get media coverage.

Stage 3: Blocking, The Art of Enragement
Using Your Flock Controller as a Bludgeon

Once you have had some time to explore the social world, you may run into a noticeable pattern of social blocking. For instance, a Twitter user may insult someone. Then, the insulted person responds or accuses them of the exact behavior. The insulter reports them as spam and blocks them. The classic example is political Liberals calling others racist while simultaneously engaging in racists activities; or political Conservatives calling for small government while voting for huge government surveillance programs like the Patriot Act. Neither of these so called liberals or conservatives are real. While it is possible they are just some crazy person, chances are they are part of a calculated propaganda team designed to group with your flock.

Why Would They Do This?
Simple, they can play a role in silencing dissenting speech to your client's advantage. If the hypocritical activist can get enough real users sufficiently enraged, their emotional subconscious takes over enough to report a dissenter as a spamming trigger, or a *Spam Slam* inside of Twitter, silencing the opposing political speech.

After enough of these fake spam reports go to the Twitter software, it will place the user into Twitter jail, temporarily limiting the dissenting speech. This is an old tactic, nonetheless, it can be used to effectively silence the wagging tongues. After all, we would not want our followers to question our cause.

Pro Tip

Once you convince your flock that your opponent is a racist or bigot, it's time to whip them into a frenzy and deploy them like shock troops. Simply unleash them as free speech protesters and allow them to reign hell to stop your target from speaking.

**This is an effective and substantial part
of any Modern Propaganda campaign.**

Stage 4: Putting Your Social Flock to Work
Berating, Belittling, and Exploiting

Now that you understand how to build a social flock, it's important to put it to work. I typically will start by searching around Twitter to locate a currently trending topic or event. These trending topics will inevitably be followed by media outlets who support a particular political party or cause. This is convenient as it makes it easy to leverage a news outlet that supports or opposes your issue, which to our delight, simplifies the task at hand as this creates a win-win situation.

When a news outlet opposes your political agenda by posting a biased story, expectedly, a group of users will call them out. Therefore, you can join the group by participating in discrediting the news organization for gaining new followers. However, when a news outlet publishes a politically favorable news report, one can support and embrace the media outlet. In the world of Modern Propaganda, we are concerned with growing your flock and achieving the desired outcome. Therefore, use your flock controller to stoke outrage whether you believe in it or not.

Pro Tip
It's best to create two distinct flock personas in order to capitalize on and gather followers from the left and right spectrum. This way you always have a political, expedient flock ready and willing to go into a mob mentality. These followers can be used like a media bludgeon if you should need them.

No need to worry about journalist's standards on the Internet since the news reporters don't care, nor should you. It's simply not a concern of this generation. News reporting, speed and sensationalism are the new standards. Give the people what they want and you will create flocks that last forever.

> *Many journalists are lazy and look to you*
> *to supply them with the news they need to do their job.*
> *Take advantage of this.*

The Celebrity Experiment
#CelebrityExperiment

Yes, looks are important. Yes, popularity matters. And, yes, people love to follow celebrities on and off line. Most propagandists know this, but many, including marketers and business leaders, have no idea what's involved in getting a celebrity to follow and interact with you on social media.

The allure is compelling but getting the wrong celebrity, not only risks their reputation, it can undermine your efforts to influence others. The other thing to keep in mind is celebrities are people. Some are cool, some are not so cool, but they all have problems, friends and lives like you or me. Being a celebrity is what they do, not really who they are in many cases. Some of my favorites celebrities have really taught me a lot about the business and what it means to be respectful to fans. One celebrity in particular, whom I shall keep anonymous, taught me some great lessons in humility. However, at the end of the day, what I discovered is many propagandists have no idea how to leverage or work with these great assets. This is why I ran a test called The #CelebrityExperiment, which is, in fact, more of a propaganda methodology than an actual experiment. This is also a Hashtag we trend from time to time on Twitter.

Socially Savvy or a PR Pawn? The Celebrity Experiment

To simplify, we start with the assumption that there are two types of celebrities. Type 1 works only with large talent agencies, and type 2 works with smaller ad agencies or directly through the use of an agent. First, we determine which type of celebrity we want via examining their social media profile, mostly on Twitter, to determine if they are self-managing their social media or not. This is important because if you can tell it's a PR person then they are not doing a very good job. This also says that the celebrity is really not connected with the fans enough to use social media as an influential tool. This is not to say that a celebrity using a PR person is bad, it's just that if they do not understand how to manage a PR person to make their persona seamless in social media, they are not going win online effectively.

Friend or Foe?

Next, we examine friendliness. Here is where you are faced with a dilemma. The real objective is to calibrate how well a celeb interacts with social media fans. Determine if they are super busy, just cold and detached, or perhaps guarded because of previous issues with fans, like stalking. Fans can be fanatical after all.

Interact and Attract

An important next stage of the #CelebrityExperiment is interaction. You need to start to interacting with the celebrity. Some choose flattery, others choose cunning. I prefer to be myself with humor and ask questions which I am sincerely curious about. Amazingly, you learn they are people and like all people they live in a world of ups and downs. At this phase, your abilities and skill inside of social media will be put to the test. Off topic questions are always catchy and endorsements of a product they are promoting will surely get you noticed. Wines, perfumes, books and clubs are all up for the taking. Who cares if you're not a woman using herbal women's shampoo, you love it and it's the best product ever made. Be careful here. There is a fine line between being an influencer and fan. You want to land squarely in the gray.

The celebrities who are immersed in the reality TV world will tend to be the most active in the promotion arena; and will eagerly seek new products and services to endorse as their careers tend to be short lived and burn hot, yet, burn out.

Drama, Drama

In addition to promotion, they thrive on drama because drama equals eyes and reach in the market. If you find two celebrities talking bad to each other, or perhaps, caught in some kind of love triangle, pick a side and stoke the flames. This will win you points with the celebrity or PR person, as you both know good drama equals good ratings and good ratings equal good money. The cold hard reality is if you win the audience, you win the game. Even better, as you help your celebrity win the audience he or she may hand you an ounce of respect.

Did they retweet you? Great! Did they tweet back? Better! Did they follow you? Excellent! If any of these occur it's time to continue with your interactions. Don't do anything creepy like DM them to death, at least not yet.

A "Friendship" Born

It's amazing! I can't believe it! I've been followed by celebrity Y! Ok, good job, now keep your cool and get ready for the long haul. This is where a long and steady drip, drip, drip of social media interaction pays off. By long, I mean many years. It's also the time to start to cultivate many other potential candidates for your campaign. The reason you cultivate and evaluate a number of celebrities is for two reasons. On one hand, you both may be interested in an actual friendship. Yes, it happens. On the other hand, they may not be interested in doing business with you. Celebrity friendship is subjective. Unless you are having morning coffee together you will really never know if they are your friend or using you to spread their own propaganda. It's most likely the latter but if it's mutually beneficial, who cares.

That being said, if you find a connection and think this particular celebrity will be a good fit it's time to follow the yellow brick road and participate in the lie of the celebrity influencer dynamic.

Ride the Wake of The Celebrity Experiment

This is Modern Propaganda. We are looking for influence and to influence. The soft kind of influence that sways minds, targets the masses, and subtly erodes the positions of your enemies. Will a celebrity promote your product, or blindly endorse you? No. However, by tweeting and interacting with you to gain followers, you, in turn, gain credibility with your fellow social media plebs. Depending on the caliber of the celebrity, one re-tweet can create a fire storm of interactions and follows. Each mind, ripe for being a mini mega phone to your cause.

Digital Graphite, Digital Education
Training the Next Generation of Social Warriors

Get your #2 lead pencils ready. Well, in fact, pencils are now made of graphite, not lead, but who cares. While the current system of education is still entrenched in the 19th century factory learning module, the bulk of our youth is actively learning online and through digital means.

IPhones, Kindles, tablets and streaming video are in; hands on learning is out. Well, it's not out completely in all cases. Private education systems, such as Montessori schools, have created a modern learning environment where the focus on holistic learning has managed to overcome this trend, but this is not the norm. The vast majority of youth are shuffled like cattle into overcrowded schoolrooms 5 days a week where they dream of escaping from their 19th century factory prison.

So what does this have to do with Modern Propaganda?

The answer is everything. Death is the most disruptive technology of all. Therefore, the youth are the future. If you can influence the youth; you can influence the future. This is not a new phenomenon, rather, a centuries old concept dating back to Spartan society where the youth were trained to be soldiers. Now, as with times of old, the youth can be made into political soldiers to move and steer as you desire.

And, while the form of propaganda under the guise of political correctness has been drilled into the modern U.S. student's psyche, this has not been fully effective. This is because the education system is out dated by over 100 years or more, and it lacks the strong digital component which represents the vast majority of information a student receives. A student will no longer simply be able to be shown one side of an issue and then blindly accept it as proof. Even at a young age where the students are most malleable and subject to believe in a teacher's point of view, without digital influence, this steering of belief does not fully take hold.

This creates an opportunity for disruption. Disruption, not only from a business point of view, but disruption from a Modern Propaganda point of view. As propagandists teaching our young students, we know our opponents are wicked, evil, bigoted, racists, steeped in sexism. The young must be wired to combat this since only the vigor and enthusiasm of youth is enough to win your cause. Therefore, to make the propaganda of education take hold, you must embrace the digital world.

When choosing a teacher or influencer for cultivating youth, you will find that religious zealots are extreme and garner ill-will; socialists have had some success but the effect on society has been dismal; and authoritarian leaders are short lived. Therefore, finding a balance of Conservative yet Progressive seems to have the most profound effects. The Conservative nature takes advantage of the will to succeed while bettering oneself, and the Progressive nature takes advantage of the perception of bettering society.

Hash Tag, You're It
Hash Tagging Your Way to a Stereotype
When it comes to labels and people, the general understanding is that people do NOT like to be labeled or stereotyped. This is false especially when it comes to the Internet and social media.

People like to be labeled. In fact, virtually every social media profile you read is nothing more than a constructed manifestation of a manufactured persona that is personally labeled. By labeling someone you are helping their ego solidify their own self-image, thereby helping you to gain followers and influence.

The entire premise of Twitter, for example, is based on labeling in the form of #HashTags. Entire trends are created around these labels.

So, go ahead and label, stereotype and participate in the madness. Labeling is a necessary part of Modern Propaganda. On one hand you satisfy the psychological need to be labeled and stereotyped, and on the other hand, you get your message through the noise.

Obviously, the entire idea of labeling quickly backfires if the label does not fit what a person believes he or she is. Therefore, this is to be avoided.

4
CONTENT RINGS & PRESS NETWORKS

How do you make the news? You produce it, speak it and fabricate it until they love you. After all, news is quite simply a manufactured perception of events. The Internet is ideally suited for this function.

Today's consumer not only understands modern news is nothing more than a left or right perspective on a story, in fact, they demand to be fed the biased view to sustain their own perception of reality. Fox News, The Huffington Post, MSNBC and online outlets like Salon all facilitate biased news that helps drive their own political agendas. And you know what? The viewers love it!

Is this wrong? Maybe, but it is also virtually impossible for a news outlet to function without a point of view. Even if they attempt to be politically neutral on a story, they inherently have a bias. The phenomenon has become so invasive on the Internet that news and political theater can be impossible to distinguish.

Your job is not to decide if biased news coverage is right or wrong but to exploit it to achieve your goals. I mean, why not? The media outlets are exploiting you for large profits. Therefore, it is necessary for you to exploit them to get the 'truth' of your cause out on the public stage.

Going from Digital to Real
One of the most critical parts of your propaganda machine is your private content distribution network. Before we get into the building of this model, I want to share a story. Perhaps, many of you may be skeptical that propaganda exists in today's digital world.   Or perhaps, you understand that most things on the Internet should be looked at skeptically but you believe those influences never effect the real world. I used to joke with my staff that a thousand years from now the digital

graffiti we post today will pop up on the Internet like an ancient cave painting. So, we decided to run an experiment based on a bug we found.

In 2014, our staff discovered a bug in Google Maps where they could log into Google Maps semi anonymously and re-name or name buildings, ponds and city bounds. This, on it's own, would not be an issue but we quickly found that other providers relied on Google Maps as their source of information for publishing. *(This was recently addressed by Google once someone exploited the map system to draw a large image of the Google Android urinating on the Apple logo.) However, many things, including Google Maps, are crowd sourced which means large holes are still present if you know where to look. This is always the case in a crowd sourced environment.)*

The experiment went as follows: one of my staff members logged into Google with an account, picked a body of water and renamed it in Google Maps. The name was chosen after one of his childhood friends, Murphy. He renamed a body of water to Murphy's Pond in Clifton Park, NY 12065. This is simple enough. However, to our amazement, within days our model was proven true. On a highway adjacent to the pond a car accident occurred. This was followed by multiple news and media outlets such as the Times Union, NEWS10 ABC: Albany, New York News and many others covering the story with the fictitious name, Murphy's Pond.

Some Headlines were:

> **"Men risk their lives to save burning man in Clifton Park"**,
> Times Union website
> *NEWS10 ABC: Albany, New York News*
>
> *"An oil-slick containment strip and burned ground remain on the shore of **Murphy's Pond** on Barney Road in Clifton Park on Saturday, Aug. 9. 2014, where a car crashed and caught fire Friday, Aug. 8, 2014."*[1]

Adam Myers `14 Risks Life in Heroic Rescue Attempt

"As the starting goalie for Siena's men's soccer team, Adam Myers '14 made his share of big saves before. But nothing could have prepared him for what transpired Friday night.

Myers (Ballston Spa, N.Y.) had just finished golfing 9-holes at Barney Road Golf Course in Clifton Park when his day took a dramatic turn.

He was driving slowly down residential Barney Road just after 8 p.m. when he saw a car driving in the other direction filled with smoke. Myers turned to see the car careen through a parking lot, and then down a shallow ravine into **Murphy's Pond**.

He didn't hesitate to react, sprinting toward the burning vehicle.

"It was like something you see in the movies," Myers said when reached on his cell phone Monday morning. "The cabin of the car was completely engulfed in flames.""[2]

Official State Documents
The simple act of reporting Murphy's Pond was soon followed by its inclusion into an official state document:
http://www.saratogacountyny.gov/wp-content/uploads/2015/01/January-20-Meeting.pdf

According to the Saratoga County website www.saratogacountyny.gov:

> On January 20th, "Mr. Barrett read a proclamation entitled 'Honoring Adam Myers, Mike Campanella and Deputies Jonathan Grady and Jeffrey O'Connor for their heroic rescue efforts at Murphy's Pond in the Town of Clifton Park.'"

The point is that the web now has the power to influence the real world and even change official state documents that are edited and published. What this shows is that we are on a disruptive communication wave just like newspapers, radio and TV were in days past. Few times in the history of mass communication do you have the ability to disrupt, influence and sculpt the future as you do now.

Wiki Me Not
Smacking the Facts Out of You

Of all the strategies, this is perhaps one of the most effective forms of digital propaganda you can leverage. Wikipedia has become the default encyclopedia for much of the world, and more importantly, the default information source that many smartphone apps use to display information when users ask a question or need help. As with many things, Wikipedia's strength is also its weakness. It is edited by a "Do-ocracy" which makes it possible to keep vast amounts of information updated. Conversely, because it is edited by so many users it is impossible to keep tight central control of the content. The environment has become ripe for political activists willing to subject the masses to their sometimes twisted version of the truth; and we love it. All propagandists must learn to embrace this ability and slowly become a trusted "Wiki Author" so that you may plant the seeds of decent and propaganda. The more you are trusted, the more the members of the Wiki community who regulate the body, will overlook your calculated edits, provided you are subtle. Wiki editing is so powerful, yet, it is a finely woven craft where you sow the seeds over time. Those who use Wiki as a bludgeon, instead of a scalpel to simply get revenge, will surely be caught.

> ### *Slowly edit wiki pages until you gain trust, then you can strike.*

One of my favorite examples is Ben Koo's article on Awfulannouncing.com:

> ### *Guilt by Wikipedia: How Joe Streater became falsely attached to the Boston College point shaving scandal*
>
> *"Joe Streater was not part of the Boston College point shaving scandal that was popularized this week by ESPN's latest 30 for 30, Playing for The Mob. That's about all I can tell you about Joe Streater.*

I don't know if he's alive, I don't know where he lives if he is indeed alive, I don't know if he's married or if he has kids, I don't know what careers and jobs he's had along the way, and I don't know why he left Boston College early in 1978 during a successful freshman year on the basketball team. Attempts to contact Streater this week both through Boston College and alumni groups were unsuccessful.

For years, Streater has been falsely linked with one of the greatest scandals in the history of college sports. Streater was 100% not involved in the point shaving scandal despite the fact media organizations including Sports Illustrated, The Associated Press, local media outlets, and Boston College blogs say he did. Here's the AP version:

> *"BC basketball players Rick Kuhn, Joe Streater and Jim Sweeney were persuaded to fix nine Eagles games during the season. Kuhn and two money men were handed 10 years each in prison."*

Streater wasn't even on the team or in school at that time the point shaving took place in the 1978-1979 season, an observation that is occasionally made on message boards and comment sections, but is quickly dismissed given the abundance of articles stating that Streater was among those involved.

So how does a man's name become besmirched to the point where his false indiscretions are constantly retold to the point they become common fact in today's media?

The answer – Wikipedia.

From August 2008 until yesterday, the Wikipedia page for the point shaving scandal at Boston College named Streater as a participant in the scandal over five times. Nobody caught the error or at least corrected it until this week (probably because of the film's airing or perhaps some of the outreach I was doing spurred some movement). Over time it snowballed to the point where Streater's involvement became prevalent online and thus was just accepted as fact. It's not."[3]

Even slight factual changes can have great results on your propaganda efforts. As they say in warfare, "history is written by the victor."

Building Your Own Future

The technology industry is full of individuals who can convincingly lead an organization to its destruction. Everyone is a "tech person" or has some magical formulation. The vast majority of these "tech visionaries" are incompetent at best and liars at worst. However, they can be convincing to even seasoned professionals. I call these individuals the *"Qualified" Unqualified*.

When you're ready to build your propaganda machine, assuming you don't already have a private distribution network or own a media outlet, you must have your team build it. This can be extremely complex, therefore, use caution when hiring and avoid choosing the *"Qualified" Unqualified*. Therefore, in this chapter, we are going to build a simple content network I call, *The Broadcaster*.

The Broadcaster (See Basic Diagram)

The Broadcaster is one of my favorite content network designs. This content network alone consists of over 1,500 individual distribution points combined with a deep syndication network and much more. The structure is that of a giant propaganda megaphone.

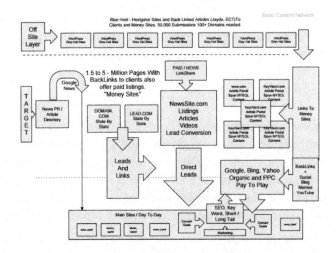

Tier 1: Master Websites - Media Sites

These are your real websites and the main targets to which you wish to drive traffic, users and press. These are also the sites that will have the best search results and page rank on the Internet. The artwork and content should be extremely professional and have a sophisticated look and feel. At a glance, the user should fully trust your cause and believe this is the trusted source for the topic. I use this simple formula:

High Search Rank + Trust = Success

In fact, your sites can become so useful you may find media and outside groups quoting your work. This is perfect as it creates evangelism around your subject matter and saves you countless man hours. You may find you even establish contacts in these media outlets who are, not only eager for new content, but will actively participate in your cause.

Tier 2: 250 Top Level Domain Names

Start by having the content team pick 3-5 naming conventions to split your domain names. Typically, I start by purchasing 150-200 top level domains.

A fairly standard mix for your naming convention is by Cause, Media, Key Term and Organization.

Example website names might be.
- www.pretendnonprofit.com
- www.causenews.com
- www.causemedia.com
- www.causekeyterms.com
- www.causepowergroup.com

Make sure when purchasing the names to cloak your Whois record and deploy the domains on multiple Internet IPs and subnets. This is essential to disrupting Internet search bots from flagging you.

Next, you will install your favorite blogging software into each domain, automating along the way. Have your programming staff build out or buy blog posting software.   I prefer to use a mix of WordPress, Drupal and custom platforms. There are some advanced prebuilt systems on the market that can be used for cost savings. However, if you have high security needs, an exclusive custom built system is the only way to go.

Tier 3: RSS Syndication
It is common for most blogging platforms to have RSS syndication. Using a mix of robots and staff you will embed the RSS link into the syndication websites. I like to work with 50 or more providers.

It is preferable to set the website you're syndicating to post at random times. This gives it the appearance of being more genuine. Additionally, it is useful to incorporate syndicated feeds from 3rd party news sites that carry similar topics, this too, adds to the credibility.

Services like Feed Burner allow for you to build elaborate content distribution chains from your basic RSS feed.

Tier 4: Primary Social Networks
Online there are only a handful of primary social networks that will help build the foundation of your social media reach. These are Facebook, Twitter, LinkedIn, Tumblr, and G+.

Facebook and G+ will allow you to create business pages to interact with your user groups. Additionally, Facebook has a publisher feature which will allow you to post custom white papers and articles.

Postings should be from a mix of automated robots and personnel. Facebook, in particular, will require that you engage, and in many cases, debate real users.

Tier 5: Web 2.0 Social Networks
Unknown to many, a large number of secondary social networks exist. It is simple to write a series of robots which act like people and post to these networks. Some of these include Tumblr, Wet Paint and more. Keep in mind that these networks tend to attract very specific targeted, niche markets. However, they can help contribute to your main website's search exposure.

Tier 6: Social Bookmarking

For every post of content you make, a web page is generated. During the process of submitting content, you will store these web page addresses in a database. You will then randomly submit these to social bookmarking sites like Reddit for users to find and follow.

Tier 7: Blog Ring

The blog ring is nothing more than disposable domains and hosting accounts that you can use to publish news stories, content and messaging to your targets. These blogs can be mass produced using standard WordPress scripts and databases. Many of these blogs will never be found by your users but they act as a catalyst in pushing your main sites higher in the search results. Build these and throw them away once you are finished.

Tier 8: Paid Press Release Services and Traditional Media

Many paid press release services exist on the Internet. They have existing relationships with numerous local TV websites and targeted media outlets by region. While it is unlikely that these paid media services will get picked up in an actual local newspaper, Google News, a powerful driving media force, does tend to carry the releases, giving them credibility.

Building your own press release system is certainly possible. To do so, you can buy existing lists of editors and journalistic contacts from places like Mondo Media, or research them using the Internet media library. The basic premise is simple since each town or country across a given region has a mix of TV and Newspapers. Simply go to each of their websites and look up the contact names and reach out to them in a journalistic fashion. Keep in mind, there are over 15,000 Newspaper and TV media outlets in the U.S. We have included a list of the top 100 newspapers with websites in the Appendix titled, Thoughts on Targetable Media Outlets. For a quick look, here are the leaders.

TOP 14 NEWSPAPERS
1. Wall Street Journal
2. USA Today
3. New York Times
4. Los Angeles Times
5. San Jose Mercury News
6. New York Post
7. Washington Post
8. New York Daily News
9. Chicago Sun-Times
10. Chicago Tribune
11. Dallas Morning News
12. Denver Post
13. Newsday
14. Houston Chronicle

Before I leave the subject of PR or press strategies, I have found that the most fruitful time to maximize press is during the months of July and August. My observations indicate that reporters may be less inundated with press releases and more willing to look at your story. City councils and governments tend to be out of session during these times which leaves reporters digging for news to fill the void. Leverage this time period of the summer to your advantage; after all, if you don't, another certainly will.

Tier 9: Paid News Content
It's a known fact that it is difficult to make money on the Internet selling subscriptions. While people have started to accept the idea of paying for content, the Internet was founded on the principle of open and free media. That deeply ingrained mentality will not erode any time soon. Publishers have discovered that they can make large sums of money with a product called native advertisements.

Unlike simply placing a banner or ad on the news website, native advertising allows you to produce your own content which is published on the media outlet's site but often appears like a news story or article rather than an advertisement. Many times, the article will have a small watermark of your firm to distinguish it from actual news. However, plenty of high value backroom deals are conducted which allow you to become a "contributor". The result: your article appears as if it's an in house news story thus tricking the reader, and voila, your credibility rate and reader engagement are much higher.

It is true, many editors position themselves as above approach and will even refer to this method of paid news manufacturing as unethical.

Is it? The answer is no, not at all, especially when they get a paycheck which many gladly take. These same writers that will look down on this method of news production seem to have no issues participating in the group think mentality that drives current journalistic schools of thought. Therefore, before you have any guilt, think about this: there are over 350 million people in the U.S.A., yet, a limited group of agenda driven news stories are presented as fact each day. This leaves millions of stories and points of view untouched by the so called journalistic community.

This strategy gives you a voice and a platform for your message in a landscape of money, corruption and deception that would otherwise be a barrier for your message. Trust cash to get your message out.

Trust and Fear
Interestingly enough, even unsurprisingly, high ranking government officials can benefit from paid media as well. In this case, instead of money, they can leverage trust or intimidation, which when combined with a skilled PR firm, becomes a very valuable tool of influence.

Following is the recent trust rank of media outlets from PEW Research. This can be used as a guide for distributing and investigating propaganda topics. Keep in mind, many of the politically right media personalities tend to have a lower trust rank. However, this is because their audience reach and share is significantly larger in scope and crosses the left and right spectrum of viewers, whereas the left leaning shows have very little market share and capture only the hard political left spectrum.

Pay special attention to how the left wing media sources have more trust. Yet, the right wing sources have a much larger audience. So, as a digital analyst, you must ask how they arrived at these numbers.

Trust Levels of News Sources by Generation

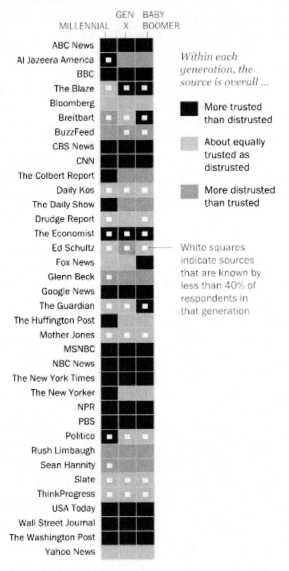

Within each generation, the source is overall ...

More trusted than distrusted

About equally trusted as distrusted

More distrusted than trusted

White squares indicate sources that are known by less than 40% of respondents in that generation

American Trends Panel (wave 1). Survey conducted March 19-April 29, 2014. Q20, Q21a, Q21b. Based on online adults.

PEW RESEARCH CENTER

http://www.journalism.org/2015/06/01/millennials-political-news/pj_15-06-01_millennialmedia13/

Now, ask yourself why should you hand the power of your agenda over to someone who may not embrace your truth, when instead you can control the truth.

> **Modern Propaganda is not just about controlling the message; it's about creating reality.**

Wielding Power

For those of you who may still doubt that Modern Propaganda is in use, I leave this chapter with a story and submit the following case of Google *vs. Mississippi Attorney General.*

Imagine if a powerful attorney general was to target your company or livelihood? This happened to Google. Fortunately for them, they had the resources to fight back.

Sued by Google, a State Attorney General Retreats
-The New York Times

By ERIC LIPTON and CONOR DOUGHERTY DEC. 19, 2014

"Attorney General Jim Hood of Mississippi on Friday agreed to call a "time out" in his fight with Google after the Internet giant filed a lawsuit accusing him of conspiring with the movie industry.

The move by Mr. Hood, who has been one of Google's most outspoken critics, came only hours after the company asserted in its lawsuit that Mr. Hood had been improperly influenced by major Hollywood studios that are trying to crack down on the distribution of pirated movies on the Internet.

The lawsuit, filed in federal court in Mississippi, had also questioned the authority of state law enforcement officials to regulate Internet service providers....

.... Mr. Hood issued a 79-page subpoena in October, asking that the company turn over information about its search engine and sales of illegal drugs, pornography and other materials. He suggested that the company was knowingly profiting from such sales and demanded a response from Google by early January.

For several years, Google has been involved in legal wrangling with Mr. Hood and other attorneys general as the states tried to use their consumer protection authorities to push the company to crack down on such transactions. The states argued that Google benefited because the seller's advertised on the search engine.

Emails and other records obtained by The New York Times — and which were stolen from Sony by hackers — showed how the movie industry, through a nonprofit group it funded, had hired the former attorney general from Mississippi, whom Mr. Hood used to work for, to put pressure on Mr. Hood to go after the company."[4]

Variety magazine wrote (see appendix for link to article):
Google Sues to Block Mississippi Attorney General's Probe, Alleging Ties to MPAA[5]

Heavy.com wrote (see appendix for link to article):
Google vs. MPAA Showdown: 5 Fast Facts You Need to Know[6]

These seemingly innocent headlines are anything but innocuous and represent a seismic shift and windfall in the propaganda industry. Government officials not only hire PR firms to do their bidding but do so openly. I use the word *windfall* with the caveat that one must execute the plan properly using modern techniques.

As Stephanie Dube Dwilson from Heavy.com eloquently summarized in the case of Google vs. Mississippi Attorney General:

"1. Google Sued Attorney General Jim Hood, Suspecting He Was Working with the MPAA

2. The Emails Included a Plan for the MPAA to Fund Fake, Anti-Google Stories in the Media

3. The Plans Involved a Google Investor Coming Forward and Demanding Reform

4. The Next Step Would Be to Have Hood Submit a Detailed, Complex Subpoena

5. The Plan Called for a PR Firm to Handle the Details Under the Guise of Being a Concerned Non-Profit"[7]

The Basic Playbook

Stephanie's writings revealed and uncovered the most basic propaganda playbook used in today's world. The step by step illustration represents "propaganda" at its finest. However, it is not "modern" as it lacks a strong central digital focus which would be needed to achieve success for the Attorney General who was attempting to target Google.

Accordingly, Google was able to learn of this simplistic plot and clearly illustrate to a federal judge that there had been correspondence between the Mississippi Attorney General and lobbyists for the movie industry.

The New York Times reported:

> *"U.S. District Judge Henry T. Wingate ruled blocking Hood's investigation of Google in March, the Mountain View, California, company pressed its attempt to obtain copies of Hood's correspondence with the Motion Picture Association of America. The Internet giant says Hood is part of a covert campaign by movie studios to use legal action to achieve enhanced piracy protection that Congress has rejected. The company and others say that the association may have had input into the subpoena Hood sent Google, point to a Hood letter that the group apparently did draft, and note that former Mississippi Attorney*

> *General Mike Moore was hired by the Digital Citizens Alliance, a nonprofit group funded by movie studios and other companies."[8]*

The point of discussing this case is to demonstrate that, not only is propaganda real and impactful, but if done wrong or using 19th century methods, you will fail. Modern Propaganda is inherently digital in nature and assumes a few basic rules:

Rule 1: It is no longer effective to use 1950's style propaganda models where a politician in a position of power, such as an Attorney General, can simply imprison opponents and then have a society follow suit. This is because today's information is no longer centrally controlled. The Internet is highly effective at distributing information in a decentralized manner. This means that even if you have the legal authority to halt information, unlike the old days of centralized network TV, the information will find a way to reach the masses.

Rule 2: You should never attack a large formidable enemy directly, especially a technology company that trades in information. Modern Propaganda combines digital guerilla warfare techniques and technology to attack a superior enemy.

Rule 3: Never create or leverage a nonprofit to do your bidding such as Media Matters. It may seem like a good idea now, but eventually the political winds will change and with them so goes the IRS. Your nonprofit will eventually become subject to the same laws that apply to others.

It's Not Bias if You Control It

I once had a reporter tell me, "Hey, I have a right to my opinion too," after I criticized her for publishing a very biased political article in her Twitter account. The issue, as I saw it, was that her profile stated that she did work with the Atlantic and the AP. Both items give the impression to the average reader that she is more credible then she actually was. It also gives the reader the impression that her article was the view of the AP, regardless of calling it an opinion, as it is human nature to connect associations.

More recently, I was using my IPhone and went to open the newsfeed where I captured a great example of how to leverage the media. Most astonishing to me was that this was completely by chance. I was sitting on my porch trying to escape from the propaganda I constantly immerse myself into. While sipping a fine Dominican coffee, I swipe right on my screen pulling up the IPhone's default news stories. For a moment, I did a double take. The top two stories are fundamental attack ads against Trump, the man the media loves to hate. However, these are different as they were actually posted as news.

Newsfeed Acting on Behalf of a Political Party

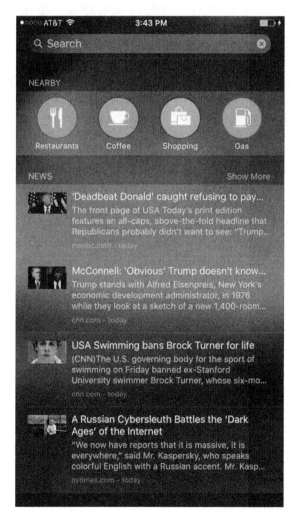

The Lesson About the News

Those who wield Modern Propaganda do so relentlessly, as they should. Then, it occurs to me how genius it is to feed the masses propaganda while they are relaxed, receptive and unaware. By blending traditional news outlets, IPhones, Androids, Google Search, and Facebook we can reach millions at their most receptive, facilitated by our most willing reporters and news partners.

Think Scale

Think about this, Tim Cook revealed at the Apple Watch conference on March 9, 2015, that Apple had sold a total of 700 million iPhones to date.[9] The number of potential people to influence is astounding.

This reach and influence is clearly on the minds of others. Recently, both Facebook and Google have been accused of manipulating the media to show stories favorable to their positions. Since this, Mark Zuckerberg the founder of Facebook, took decisive action to make sure abuse would not occur. However, this will not always be the case, as there will always be those who feel their political agenda justifies their right to spin the tale as they see fit. Modern Propaganda embraces this view. For you will always have willing reporters seeking to steer the public in one way or another and you will always have willing readers eager to accept the reality they see as theirs. This is compounded in the digital world where something like an IPhone is experienced as more than a phone, in fact, it feels like a part of our persona.

5
DIRTY LITTLE SECRETS, FAKE PEOPLE AND BOTS

We've all heard the saying, "fake it, til you make it." Well, here is a dirty little secret. On the Internet, this is doubly true. A large portion of Internet users on some of the largest networks in the world are fake. Fake, fake, fake and more fake. While companies have gotten better about weeding out the fake users, the issue is still rampant.

Bots, as they are called, are used on the Internet for everything from getting search results to scanning for exploits that a virus will use to infect a computer.

The millions of bots that swarm the Internet are ideally suited for the role of creating fake traffic and users. While most computer people notice them, the average user has no idea. For legitimate companies, bots create a very difficult problem because they skew metrics and create a situation where reports and statistics are difficult to interpret. Although, for companies that deal in the shady business of selling web traffic, bots are an essential part of the ethos.

Are fake users really bad? Sure, in the old days there was an epidemic of click fraud where bots stole money from advertising businesses by pretending to be users; that was bad. However, today's fake users, or bots, are much more sophisticated and play a valuable role in society. Many of today's bots are artificial intelligences that mimic human emotions and interactions on the Internet. As with most things, this can be used for good or malicious intent.

> *On many dating websites, bots provide social interaction to lonely people desiring companionship, while simultaneously creating a revenue stream for the business.*

One of the most famous human emulation bots on the web is the A. L. I. C. E. Bot, The Artificial Linguistic Internet Computer Entity. Its programming allows it to interpret conversations and respond accordingly to the human with whom it is interacting. Similar features have been commercialized by such places as Sitepal, which overlays human animations and images over the bot, to create an interactive experience on your website. Other significant artificial intelligence systems are the Google Prediction API and the Amazon Cloud Artificial Intelligence Service. Both of these services have the prospect of changing, not only the way computers interact and predict data for people, but, the entire landscape of mass information.

Predictive Analytics & Conversion
The future of building a mass scale propaganda model will use artificial intelligence to mimic human behavior. You will always need humans to seed and train the bots. However, instead of hiring thousands of additional staff, bots will fill the role of distributing content and social networking interaction around the web. Predictive and artificial intelligence platforms make this easy.

The machine learning and predictive analytics model enables you to create virtual emissaries who can talk pleasantries about your cause or cast doubt upon those you oppose and wish to silence. Imagine thousands of SIRI type entities with human profiles and pedigree swarming around the Internet on your behalf. Each one learning trigger points and behaviors that allows them to interact non-stop, 24 hours a day, spreading your message, interacting with your followers and seeding doubt. I see a clear, and perhaps fighting future, where expert psychologists and marketers create massive user profiles based on stimulus triggers that drive individual decision making.

So, how would we gain worldwide exposure you ask? To this question I can only give you a theoretical response, as it would require the resources of a government to accomplish. The plan would be very simple. We would build or acquire a software company that specializes in virus protection. We would give the software away for free or for a good price. Over time, millions of machines would adopt the virus protection allowing our government entity a backdoor into millions of machines. While it is true that this would also allow for spying on individual users, more so, it would allow us to deploy singular artificial intelligent bots from each machine that would slowly interact on social media over time.

The low usage of one or two bots per machine would keep the network safe from detection. Furthermore, by creating self-learning bots, the network would remain decentralized enough to offer an additional level of protection from being shut down. Now, our theoretical network of smart bots could slowly and systematically start spreading social messages over years, to gently guide the population toward the desired thinking.

While some may say this type of influencing of a population is unethical, I retort with this argument. Imagine if such a model was used to curb obesity or create a healthier population. A government could theoretically save billions, if not trillions, of dollars all for the public good. After all, many would argue it is a government's job to help a population live better and healthier, so creating such a network would in fact be in the public interest. Just ask yourself, is it so wrong to expect a healthy population? As a friend once said, "What, you don't support government healthcare? So, that means you're pro cancer."

Become the Infection to Achieve Perfection

When you wish to wage digital warfare on a state actor, it is best to start a software company and embed a backdoor, 2nd best to infiltrate a company and add a backdoor, 3rd best to create malware, and 4th best to do a denial of service attack. I say the denial of service attack will be effective but short-lived, malware will create more damage but will eventually be removed, the back door into an existing company runs the risk of getting caught. However, real software with a backdoor has the potential to take out an entire country.

Artificial Intelligence

> ## Thoughts on Artificial Intelligence:
>
> While artificial intelligence is very compelling and presents a future path for Modern Propaganda, we still find that one of the most effective ways forward is to simply infect user's computers with Adware. The goal is to compel the uneducated to go to a website or download software that injects a backdoor for your use. Once you have control of this type of network, you can do anything from artificially manipulating statistics to clicking on ads for monetary gain. The most devious of these programs will actually capture and reroute user's actions, such as, filling out a contact form and sending the data to a 3rd party. This is an effective but short term and potentially illegal strategy that may result in prison time, as Virus software companies and governments frown on such programs.

With artificial intelligence, we can now influence entire populations and lead thought for the next 100 years.

So what happens when people debate or interact with a propaganda bot? Well, we all know IBM Watson, *a question answering computer system capable of answering questions posed in natural language, developed in IBM's DeepQA project by a research team led by principal investigator David Ferrucci.* Many AI's can beat some of the best chess players in the world. However, even the best AI's have been tripped up when trying to talk to or debate an emotionally charged human, capable of non-linear thought.

This propaganda dilemma has been solved by the introduction of artificial intelligence using neural networks. With these, we can create systems that take our base line of user data and responses, and begin a constant refinement, based on actual user interaction. Over time, our AI's can, not only act like humans, but can think ahead and out debate them online. In a world of avatars, fake profile photos, and nobody really knowing who is on the other side of an Internet conversation, this is ideal.

On one hand, you can bombard and steer the targets with masses of propaganda. On the other hand, you can derail your enemy with unemotional wit. These bots prove to be both useful and disposable provided the correct technical team is in place to execute the plan.

As for those who fear a future of artificial intelligence robot's interacting with people, I disagree. The bots harbor no emotion and therefore are not able to be provoked to physical violence, unlike an actual human. This has the distinct advantage of control. You can simply shut them off or press a reset button when necessary.

However, I do suppose the great minds like Hawking and Musk have a smidgen of a point when they say that an artificial intelligence could be dangerous if allowed to grow unregulated. Like a person, the bot may attempt to achieve an outcome in an unpredictable fashion. To this extent, I do not think it is worth fearing over. I would say move forward and build an army of bots. Power and influence are difficult to gain, yet easy to destroy. Therefore, if you should need to destroy your army you can do so.

6
FAKE OUTRAGE, ENEMY LISTS & VIRAL LIES

So, what is an enemies list? Well, it can be anything from groups of people you are politically against, to nation by nation warfare. Making an enemy list is your choice.

What I will tell you is that the most common form of an enemy list is business to business attacks. I find there are a few common reasons this occurs. Number one, a business accustomed to business in the real world hires a digital marketing agency and fails to pay or steals their intellectual website property. The digital agency, usually consisting of coders and overseas staff, realizes traditional legal means are not an option so they take matters into their own hands. Number two, a business hires a black hat digital marketing agency who takes out competitors to gain search positions. Number three, although less common, but more frequent during election cycles, NGO will hire or recruit fleets of trolls to target political opponents allowing an element of separation from the candidate or party they support.

Regardless of the reason, we will cover how these techniques are done so you may better understand and detect them when they occur. Assuming you have an enemy list ready, you must learn to cover your trail. This is done by proxy.

Using a Proxy
In the older IRC (Internet Relay Chat) and other Dark Net zones you can hire for almost everything. While this can be useful, it also exposes you to dangerous situations where coders can quickly turn on you. Therefore, the first thing you need to do is set up your own proxy, which is simply a server that masks your activity and makes it look like you're coming out of a particular location. One of the most well-known proxies is HMA or Hide My Ass. Another way to mask your trail is to set up

banks of virtual machines. However, it should be noted that everything leaves a trail of some type as computers have mac addresses, chip identifications, etc. which companies like to embed with super cookies. While simplistic in nature, proxies allow some protection.

Each time a person uses a computer, make sure they set their web browser to private and pick a proxy that is close in proximity to the target. Constant vigilance must be adhered to and detailed records of fake account usage must be kept in order to be protected from unwanted detection.

Now, we are ready for our first attack which I call a *smear*. In fact, the technique is also referred to as *Auto Generated Slander* and was pioneered by leading liberal Dan Savage against Republican opponent Rick Santorum in the United States. According to Wikipedia:

> "The campaign for the neologism "santorum" started with a contest held in May 2003 by Dan Savage, a sex columnist and LGBT rights activist. Savage asked his readers to create a definition for the word "santorum" in response to U.S. Senator Rick Santorum's views on homosexuality, and comments about same sex marriage. In his comments, Santorum had stated that "In every society, the definition of marriage has not ever to my knowledge included homosexuality. That's not to pick on homosexuality. It's not, you know, man on child, man on dog, or whatever the case may be." Savage announced the winning entry, which defined "santorum" as "**the frothy mixture of lube and fecal matter that is sometimes the byproduct of anal sex...**"[10]

What action did he take?
> *"He created a web site, spreadingsantorum.com (and santorum.com), to promote the definition, which became a top Internet search result displacing the Senator's official website on many search engines including: Google, Yahoo! Search, and Bing.*[11]

The story was pushed along by media outlets, like Mother Jones, resulting in Google not only ranking the website with the new definition of "santorum" higher than the political candidate website, but also auto suggesting the new topic to web searchers.

The success of the campaign was unprecedented. Many of the same techniques can be used today. After all search engines are software and software is subject to exploitation.

Let's Give this a Try
A simple way to start is by manipulating the auto suggest features of many common search engines. To do this you can have users or run bots that type search requests and appending derogatory terms. For example, a normal person might type: "What party does political candidate X belong to". You will have your fleet search for "why is political candidate X evil?" and make an associated site and content submission to your network. Over time, the search engines will begin to auto suggest, "Why is political candidate X evil". This subtle, but effective, form of propaganda can plant the necessary seed of doubt into people who may be on the fence about a subject matter. Furthermore, the more real users that click on the new auto suggested term you created the more it is shown by the search engines, creating what I call a "viral lie".

Like any good lie, a viral lie is part true and part false but all gray and subject to the delightful enjoyment of the consumer.

A Viral Lie?
This means while the readers know full well the lie, *a santorum*, is not *"the frothy mixture of lube and fecal matter that is sometimes the byproduct of anal sex"*, nonetheless, they get some type of enjoyment from the lie and are more apt to spread it, thus becoming one of your disciples. On the Internet, this becomes a digital feeding frenzy consumed by an overpowering negative vortex of hate and humiliation. People will rarely admit to participating in the frenzy, however they do, and they love it.

Data Masking: The Art of Selective Data
Another method which is widely used in the industry is called data masking. Data masking is the art of taking selective bits of digital data with the goal of demeaning or distorting a competitor's word or results. While most online search and marketing experts are highly aware of this

technique, many traditional business owners either fancy themselves digital experts or are very green and easily misled.

The standard trick businesses fall prey to occurs when they are in the market for new search engine optimization (SEO) services. The SEO professional will go to a business and say, "Look, you're not ranking for your keyword search". Then they will further punctuate their failing site by pointing out that they're only at the bottom of page 1 of search. Then the SEO will follow it up with the final nail, and say, "Look, Google says this one term of "restaurant" has 14,000 views per month." Therefore, even if the business' website is producing calls and leads, the business owner is now putty in their hands and the enemy has lost all validity.

What the SEO professional failed to mention is that this is only partially true. While it is true that you do want to always try and get the root term to search but in many cases this is not the converting term for their business, nor does it have the volume. To illustrate this point more succinctly let's take the example of a business owner who is in the mindset that business growth is unlimited and therefore susceptible to the promises of shady salespeople.

Let's assume Google says there are 14,000 searches a month for the key term, "x" in a single city market. This is a huge number. However, experts in marketing, with or without a digital background, know two things. One, there are not 14,000 searches for "x" in a market. There may not be that many in the entire United States, let alone a single city. And two, the search term "x" tends to be searched by fake robots from SEO agencies and the marketers themselves, not by consumers who just type "x".

What They Are Not Saying
What the so called "expert" is not telling the willingly deceived is that not only are there not 14,000 actual viable searches in a month, but that the one search term is an aggregate sum of the derivative of 1000's of combinations of "x". We refer to these categories of search as **channels**.

Furthermore, a searcher will type items like "I need an 'x'" and so on. Google understands that consumers think differently and search differently than a business person with an industry knowledge and tries to serve what is best for the consumer.

In our case, the marketer failed to also mention that Desktop search is not only rapidly becoming outdated, but, that in addition to channels, search results change by device, location, and personal usage.   In many cases, search results no longer even display the actual website, just the location and phone number which is triangulated to the website acting as a hub.

> *Whether you play the role of*
> *the unscrupulous marketer*
> *or the role of the noble truth teller,*
> *it is crucial to understand*
> *that data masking is a widely used technique*
> *and a critical tool should you need it.*

Furthermore, understanding personality types and keenly manipulating them can be to your advantage when it comes to data.

Review Falsification and Slamming
I will not spend much time on this subject as the technique is so simplistic and old fashioned in nature that it warrants little mention. One of the most popular skewing techniques businesses tend to use is falsifying reviews. Very simply they will post or have people post fake, 5 star reviews, not only giving the consumer the impression of a great outstanding business, but Google tends to reward such behavior, so who can blame them. The other side of the coin is that competitors will "review slam" an opponent, giving them a series of poor reviews that may not be accurate.

Recently, Amazon began suing users posting false reviews just to stem this epidemic.

A Story by Ben Fox Rubin of Cnet sums it up:
Amazon sues alleged reviews-for-pay sites.

"The company has sued four separate sites this week, but only named one person so far linked to any of these sites.

Amazon has filed suit against four websites that allegedly sell phony product reviews that are placed on its main site, Amazon.com, marking the first time the company has taken legal action against such practices.

The Seattle-based online retailer filed the suit Wednesday in a Washington state court against a California man, Jay Gentile, who allegedly runs BuyAzonReviews.com, as well as several unknown parties running three other sites: BuyAmazonReviews.com, BayReviews.net and BuyReviewsNow.com.

"While small in number, these reviews threaten to undermine the trust that customers, and the vast majority of sellers and manufacturers, place in Amazon, thereby tarnishing Amazon's brand," Amazon said in the suit.

Despite substantial efforts to stamp out the practice, an unhealthy ecosystem is developing outside of Amazon to supply inauthentic reviews," Amazon said in the suit."[12]

Therefore, if you plan on doing this, please limit your exposure, by not overdoing the fake reviews, because eventually the search engines will find a way to punish those who have excessively abused the system. If you must engage in review slamming, apps like Burner allow you to get disposable phones that can be used to setup Gmail accounts. You can also use burn phones and hire overseas staff who are very skilled on these techniques.

Keep in mind, you will also need to bypass Google's image recognition software when setting up G+ profiles to use in the reviews. The way to do this is to buy stock photos from places like Think Stock and apply pixilation or a blur to the image before uploading the profile image. It's always better to be safe.

Category Tagging

Another technique is re-categorization of a business I call *category tagging*. I have seen this occur many times in the industry while helping clients uncover why their business is not showing up in Google. Again, online marketers or search companies are the main culprits of this behavior. The premise is simple. Using a Google map maker tool, they simply go in and change the category a business searches for. I have seen lawyers become pet shops and acupuncturists. Attacks of this nature tend to be less frequently targeted toward individual businesses, and more often at a competitor, with the goal of removing them from the search results so that the marketer's clients come to page one. Less competition means a greater chance of having your business listed on page one of Google. Google has done better over the years to correct this situation, but it still occurs.

While you would think you can sue over this behavior, it is, in fact, rare. First, the people doing the slamming may be in a foreign country, and second, a business may not have the resources and technical acumen to prove the judiciary malice.

For those of you with the technical knowledge, I say it is better to gain the goodwill of the business by helping them, than to use your skills to harm the business owners. One must take the role of technical savoir verses executioner in these cases.

Self-Inflicted Wounds

The most common form of self-inflicted wound is from businesses that simply do not have correct, consistent contact information on the Internet. The Internet is made of robots which are experts in culling out information with lapidary skill.

It is also very common for businesses to assume the Internet is static in nature, resulting in lethargy. Why does this matter? The issue is not with the business but with the nature of sophisticated software used online. Each time companies like Google make a change, there is a chance your data, such as your address or category of your business, will be modified incorrectly. This can result in millions of dollars in lost revenue. After all, if you were looking for an eye doctor you would not choose an animal doctor would you?

Another common form of self-inflicted wounds is not being aware, or not caring about, your local political climate. In an era of Modern Propaganda this is dangerous.

The story that best illustrates this is popularly known as *The Dentist Who Killed the Lion.*

Dr. Walter J. Palmer is a dentist from Minnesota who killed the beloved, Cecil the Lion, while on safari in Zimbabwe. He and a professional hunting guide lured Cecil the Lion out of his protected habitat onto a neighboring farm where it was legal to shoot it, and so he did. Unknown to the dentist, the lion was being monitored and was, in fact, famous. The Internet proceeded to go crazy with everyone from Twitter to Tumblr communities expressing outrage. This was soon followed by many mainstream media outlets adding to the digital feeding frenzy. Now, the angry mob hungry for justice, moved on with their revenge by giving the dentist thousands of fake, negative reviews and, thus, a promising career was destroyed.

Good, you say? After all he killed a famous, protected lion. Perhaps, but more importantly it is critical that you understand the mob. You MUST not only wield it, but protect yourself from it as well.

Ready, Aim, Fire
Wielding a mob requires planting a partially true story that will get activists targeting your victim. Protecting yourself from the mob requires understanding the current politically correct issues of your time and not placing yourself in violation of that perception. If you must violate a politically correct position, you must do so and then quickly ask for forgiveness. If you are in the same political camp as those you seek forgiveness from they will forgive you; if you are not, they will not.

One may ask how such a digital media frenzy was created over a lion when just that same day children were being crucified in a barbaric manner in Syria. Then, shortly after, children were washing up on the shores of Greece while trying to escape the war zone. The answer is simple.

> *Those who are weak and easy to control will always mob with issues that are palatable in nature and pose no chance for reprisal.*

If the mob had created digital outrage over a child being crucified, it is entirely possible the outrage would have prompted a government to act with resolve; and the weak do not do this. You must master the digital mob to master your message. What do you really want? Do you want to control the mob or be controlled by it? I say it is better to control it.

> *It is better to control the mob than be controlled by it.*

Pro Tip

For the small business owner that is simply trying to run a legitimate business, I find tools like Moz Local or Yext can help streamline the process of listing your business if your time is limited. Since Google is the most popular place to view a business, you will need to set up a Google Places Account. While these tools can be used for good, they can also be used for evil. Be wary that any business can be re categorized into an industry they are not in.

Yext You to Death

One of the cool things you can do with Yext is override a competitor's listing in major online business search directories like Google Places and Yahoo without verification from the business. This means you can change the type of business they are in, the phone numbers and even the address. The effect is to cause great disruption to their search ranking in places like Google which will hit their ROI hard. As if that is not enough, only one user at a time can use Yext, so you can effectively lock the target business out of making the corrections to its own listing.

Reputation Vs. Ratings

Reputation management and fake review posting is a delicate balance. The dangers are: one it assumes that you or a client has probably done something wrong, and two, you are likely to engage in a legal form of fraud. As with all subjects of this nature it is also possible that fraud has been committed against a business and that some person with basic digital skills simply had a vendetta. Therefore, when it comes to reputation management, I say respond directly to complaints when you defend your position and use reputation management when the complaints are legitimate. This way you give yourself credibility by defending your business and bury the results when you cannot defend.

Take 'Em Out
Negative SEO, a Dark Art

One of the least talked out about strategies is called negative SEO. This highly effective strategy takes advantage of the fact that businesses have tried to cheat search engines like Google. Ironically, companies like Google believe that negative SEO does not really exist. This confluence of denial and the reality of Search providers needing to stop businesses from cheating creates the perfect storm.

How does negative SEO work? Basically, you spam a business' website with bad links. You can do this by using robots and submission tools to point shady links to your target's website. Most businesses are totally unsuspecting and are easily tanked. Another very common method takes advantage of domain pointing where you buy a domain that has known spamming issues and point it to a victim's site. By the time the victim figures out what is going on, usually though hiring a technical consultant, the damage is done.

Some will ask why you can't shut this down and just take legal action? Let me ask you. How do you enforce jurisdiction upon someone who may have hidden his identity and may live in a third world country where the law of the land is survival? Even if you succeed in shutting down the malfeasance, the search engine auditors may not believe you.

7
MEMES, GLITCHING & VIRAL VIDEO

Oh, how we love cats! In fact, we love cats so much on the Internet that businesses have been built around cats. With computing and global networking power beyond our wildest dreams, people will always post funny memes and mini videos, like Vines, on the Internet. The truth is these tiny creations provide an amusing distraction to the population that we must leverage.

Regardless of the silly nature of memes, I consider them to be one of the most powerful tools in your propaganda arsenal. As simple as tiny animations are, users can't get enough. At any given time, the Internet may latch onto one of these creations and cause it to go viral. Celebrities and political opponents alike have been benefited and harmed by these tiny digital artworks.

Imagine if you have a few photos of a political opponent making a gaffe or perhaps something a bit more risqué. This powerful snapshot in time may not be enough for a news outlet, but by having your graphic artists stick together the sequence of photography into an animated gif, you get a powerful and humiliating assault of imagery. Now, have your copy writers weave together some clever lines of text to layer on top and you have the recipe for viral success. However, to be effective, you cannot just make one version, you must make hundreds, if not thousands. After all the Internet is fickle and one never knows what will create the ultimate viral storm.

Perhaps one of the best uses of a meme I have seen is when a political action group puts a list of important historic laws on an image. The group, while not claiming the laws were exclusively passed by Republicans or Democrats, simply stamp their politically connected name on the image to infer such. While much of the population will be educated enough to understand which political party passed which historical law, many impressionable online viewers are not. They simply accept the association as historic fact, leaving the opposing political party as the enemy.

Maybe you don't believe me. Then, I simply suggest that you ask almost any politically correct, young person what President Lincoln's political party was when he freed the slaves, or what party drove the legislation to pass the civil rights movements. They will inevitably say the Democrats. While this is not factually correct it goes against the modern political messaging of today's manufactured reality, therefore, the recipient of the message will create an excuse to avoid changing their perception and believe it.

Conversely, ask any of your patriotic friends which party would better protect the United States in a time of war and they will say Republican. This too has no basis in reality but perception equals reality in today's world.

> ### *Perception equals Reality.*

Staged Memes
The examples above are trivial in nature compared to some of the highly targeted attacks by rogue individuals who, despite the title of rogue, are critical machinery to the propaganda message you must distribute. What they will do is attend a protest or gathering for a cause they oppose and display the most hateful aspect of the group. For example, they may attend a gathering and start waving a racist flag or attend a Wall Street protest and urinate on a car. A co-conspirator ensures a plethora of photographs and memes are quickly distributed online where the media will certainly follow with little or no investigation.

Truth be told, if your propaganda message is strong enough an enemy's meme will have little impact on your existing followers, even if the image was not staged. I have seen case after case where the founder of a politically substantial organization has been proven to have founded the organization with the sickest of intentions or deranged motivations. However, individuals and followers will not break rank for fear of upsetting the others. This fact makes it imperative to build your propaganda message so strong that not even truth can derail it.

Fortunately for us, in the case of newer political movements or when speaking of the indoctrinated or new followers of a political movement this staged meme has the effect of creating a lightning rod that drives recruitment passion and more importantly news stories and propaganda.

While I have not plunged too deeply into the murky world of politics and social controls, I do feel it is important to point out one of most successful propaganda ploys of our time which is purposeful division. This occurred with the Tea Party and Occupy Wall Street Movements. Now, when one views the movements they will say the Tea Party is right wing and Occupy is left wing. This was not always the case and for a short time both groups started to realize they wanted term limits, controls on legalized bribery, controls on insider trading and the removal of government from the pay to play world of business. The pattern of potential cooperation was clear on the Internet and clear to the marketing machinery of both political parties who realized this merger would completely disrupt the status quo, as the Internet had done to other big money industries. To this, I credit the meme for helping to keep the division wide and safe, otherwise, the results could have been tragic.

> *In propaganda, you must never allow two warring parties to join together.*

The rule is absolute and they must always be obeyed even if it takes applying marshal law to a population to do so. I call this the Three E Rule which says you must always keep an enemy fighting an enemy, otherwise, you risk becoming the enemy.

Meme Them Happy

When you can, it is best to make viewers happy. Memes are very useful as they create powerful messages while entertaining the viewer.

The most effective memes have no more than two lines of text and merge a well-known image with an unknown face. This taps into the unconscious mindset by letting the viewer associate the images with real world events and emotions.

While subconscious, subtle and funny memes are all targets that help turn your meme into something viral. Misleading association memes also play a powerful role in degrading an opponent's argument, while also having the powerful effect of humiliation. Misleading association, as I have come to call it, is so powerful that it should be a healthy part of your propaganda mix.

Seeding the Ground

Now that you have your artistic creations, it's time to seed the Internet. To begin with, your team will submit these creations to the Internet's image search layer. These include submissions to Pinterest, Twitter and Your Favorite social media platforms, as well as, mass submissions across your private content network. Once you have seeded the ground it's time to target groups on Facebook and Kik that may be favorable to your cause.

If your meme is compelling enough to make the viewers enraged or repulsed at the target, you may also consider submitting to 4chan. Be advised 4chan is not a place for the faint of heart and while it's true they can shame an opponent into submission they can also turn on you.

Twitter, in particular, is a powerful distribution tool for your propaganda memes. Once your meme is posted you can quickly slather your opponent with preemptive derogatory statements that are derived from one small aspect of the meme.

In a political example, if you are attacking conservatives you must call them derogatory terms like, teabagger and stupid. If you are attacking liberals, you must accuse them of trying to leverage government to gain power and take away individual rights. Neither of which are fully true. However, the point is simple, to reinforce the propaganda stereotype you have worked so hard to achieve. You must produce memes that give you this power, and by doing so you will maneuver the masses. After all everybody loves to pick a political side that fits their own perception of reality and memes are just the conduit you need to achieve these goals.

Let's Take a Look at Some of the Most Effective Memes

THE PEPPER MACE GUY MEMES
I'm a pepper. You're a pepper. She's a pepper too.

Figure 1: The Pepper Mace Guy, Example 1
Former UC Davis officer, John Pike, famous for casually pepper spraying a group of students in the face during a 2011 protest.

Considered one of the classic memes of all time, The Pepper Mace Guy, originally photographed by Reuters, brought young protesters to the forefront of our consciousness. It quickly spawned a viral explosion of classic memes that Savoy influencers used to their advantage.

Figure 2: The Pepper Mace Guy, Example 2

Credit: Detail of the image from JoeInSouthernCA / CC BY 3.0

Figure 3: The Pepper Mace Guy, Example 3
Classic Beatles Cover by Zack Malitz

Lt. Pike strolls through the Beatles' iconic Abbey Road cover casually pepper spraying Paul McCartney. This doctored image plays on the popularity of the Beatles to emphasize the callous absurdity of Pike's actions.

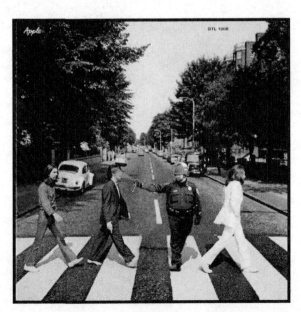

Figure 4: The Pepper Mace Guy, Example 4
George Bush Holding a Baby Getting Maced

Even though Obama was President during the 2011 protests, no viral meme would be complete without linking George W. Bush to it. After all, in the preceding years the protests were all about him. Interestingly enough, many in the Reddit community began to suspect distraction propaganda at play and reported, "Media Blackout Continues as 700+ Arrests Reported in Front of The U.S. Capitol (mrkreport.com)."

DON'T TASE ME BRO MEMES
When Questions are Asked that Don't Fit the Narrative You Get Tased

Here's a stunning example of poorly managed Modern Propaganda:
As Wikipedia reported so eloquently:
https://en.wikipedia.org/wiki/University_of_Florida_Taser_incident

"On September 17, 2007, U.S. Senator John Kerry addressed a
Constitution Day forum at the University of Florida in Gainesville, which
was organized by the ACCENT Speakers Bureau, an agency of the
university's student government. Initially allowed to ask questions after
the close of the question period, Andrew Meyer, a 21-year-old fourth-
year undergraduate mass communication student, asked a question and
was forcibly pulled away from the microphone.

He was immediately restrained and forcibly removed and was
subsequently arrested by university police. During the arrest, Meyer
struggled and screamed for help. While six officers held Meyer down,
one of the officers stunned him with a taser following Meyer's shouted
plea to the police, "Don't tase me, bro!"

Figure 5: Don't Tase Me Bro, Example 1
Andrew Meyer Being Dragged Out for Asking a Question
Credit: Unknown

Several videos of the episode were posted on the Internet, with one version reaching 7 million views on YouTube. The New Oxford American Dictionary listed "tase/taze" as one of the words of the year for 2007, popularized by the widespread use of the phrase, "Don't tase me, bro!" Meyer registered the phrase as a trademark in September 2007. "

Figure 6: Don't Tase Me Bro, Example 2

Credit: Joanahascheezburger.com

Figure 7: Don't Tase Me Bro, Example 3

Credit: Memecrunch.com

If It's Out of Control Just Apologize

What makes this meme so remarkable in terms of Modern Propaganda is that not only did it involve a well-respected U.S. Senator and a University but, ironically, the student was an actual mass media major. The almost unbelievable confluence of events created a viral storm that all parties lost control of and would like to put behind them. When this happens it may be your best course to just apologize. This is because you cannot control the digital, viral storm and the public is shocked so trying to defend the action will just stoke the flames of discontent.

THE PAJAMA BOY MEMES
Let Me Care for You

Figure 8: The Pajama Boy, Example 1

Nothing sent shivers down the spines of every day Americans like The Pajama Boy ad for a new Government Health Care Program in 2013. Single handedly conjuring up images of a creepy grown man in onesie pajamas designed for children, while sending blue collar workers a clear message they will be working for the rest of their lives to pay for this guy's care as he sits and drinks his warm cocoa. At first, many thought this ad was actually fake and released by opponents of the Health Care Bill, but it turned out to be real, opening the door to a viral storm.

Figure 9: The Pajama Boy, Example 2
by Adam Weinstein

Figure 10: The Pajama Boy, Example 3
The National Review Magazine

Dueling Narratives:

Charles C.W. Cooke writes that the "Pajama Boy" ad shows the Obamacare machine doesn't know what normal human beings are like — even as it presses to take more and more control of our lives."

Big Government's big waste was the viral message here.

Figure 11: The Pajama Boy, Example 4
I'll Care for You, Pajama Boy Strikes Back MEME by Phil Cooke

While Memes in abundance came out against the health care bill questioning the financial viability and manliness, it did not take long before supporters of the Health Care Bill came to the rescue of the bill and Pajama Boy.

A counter campaign was quickly organized which was coined the "Gruber Effect" by Propagandists. Jon Gruber, a primary Democratic architect of the health care bill, brilliantly recognized that in order to get the bill passed you must mislead the public about the true nature of the bill. He specifically refers to American voters as ill-informed or "stupid".

In October 2013, Gruber said the bill was deliberately written "in a tortured way" to disguise the fact that it creates a system by which "healthy people pay in and sick people get money". He said this obfuscation was needed due to "the stupidity of the American voter" in ensuring the bill's passage. He laid down the framework and mythology of "one party legislation" where it is required to demonize half of the American public who opposes legislation, and bribe the other half with the dream of helping others, while saving money which is in their self-interests.

Figure 12: Pajama Boy, Example 5
Pajama Boy Strikes Back
This arbitrary meme brought to you by Christ and Pop Culture Illustrator, Seth T. Hahne.

In a classic meme, counter campaign *Christ and Pop Culture* wrote: *"Pajama Boy is Everything That's Wrong with American Manhood! (and Other Misconceptions) It's poor stewardship of your time and your platform to try to turn this serious problem about healthcare into a false problem of "manhood." Thousands of uninsured (who, let me assure you, do not all fit your stereotypes) desperately need this — or some kind of reform — to work. "*

Getting Your Trump On

Figure 13: I'm a Real Newspaper Believe Me Meme
Boston Globe Goes All in on Propaganda

In The Boston Globe's Sunday edition, the newspaper's editorial board calls Trump's raucous primary campaign "deeply disturbing" and "profoundly un-American."

Nothing says credibility like creating a fake cover of your newspaper to attack a political opponent. This meme, produced by the Boston Globe, was considered genius. On one hand, the cover was *satire* so it technically did not cross political attack ad laws and, on the other hand, it was innovative and garnered a huge amount of viral attention. The meme itself exemplifies today's journalism standards and is a good example of Modern Propaganda.

Figure 14: Trump, The War Hawk

Credit: Posted in Funnyjunk.com By Anon Rare Trump Meme's

This Trump meme shows an example of painting Trump as a war hawk. While he was totally against the Iraq war and not in favor of interfering with other countries' internal struggles, it is critical if you work in propaganda politics to paint Republicans as war mongers and Democrats as peace nicks.

Figure 15: Mother Trump

Credit: Posted by threedogs-toaster

This meme shows Trump feeding his Trump flock with cash. It's not only hilarious but hits at the issue of his followers being stupid like baby birds waiting for a regurgitated meal.

If you can't beat them, demonize them.

Figure 16: Trump Chicken
A Viral Meme After Trump Turned Down Debating Bernie Sanders
Chicken Trump – Munch a bunch a crunch a munch.

This is perhaps one of my favorite Modern Propaganda memes. Not only does this tasty meme have a wonderful comedic value, the news media actually covered it as a story giving it additional credibility in the primetime propaganda feeding. This also shows that while Bernie Sanders never became the Democratic candidate, his team was remarkably adept at Modern Propaganda which goes to another point.

You can win the crowd but still lose the battle.

This occurs if you do not control the levelers of power. Ultimately, one must move the playing field of perception so that they may pass laws that are favorable to their ideals. However, that is a larger discussion. But understand this: the masses will see and hear a message as true but will always turn to pre-established rules and laws for guidance. Most are unable or unwilling to make true change as true change is difficult and requires more than screaming at others to get your point across. True change requires effort and in some extreme cases the willingness for an individual to put their lives on the line for what they believe in.

Digital Socialism Memes

Figure 17: Bernie Sanders Meme
Socialism Is Awesome!

Have an IPhone, IPad, or Android? That must mean you're a socialist.
While Sander's team mastered the use of Modern Propaganda they
were not immune from opponent's striking back. The tactic his
opponents took was to hit Sanders and his flock hard on Sander's
socialistic slant. As the example above shows, they show actual photos
from socialist countries like Venezuela where the currently collapsing
commodities, such as bread, are hard to come by and electricity is in
short supply. Never mind having a thousand dollar IPad or IPhone that
average citizens of a socialized country could only dream of. This
undermines the intelligence of his followers by suggesting that they
have no idea that the whole reason they can even use an IPhone is
because they are part of a capitalistic system. Obviously most of his
followers understand that large government run systems is not a

healthy way to live in the long term but painting the brush wide corners them. Second, it sows fear into Sander's opponents flock be showing what will happen if he is elected. Overall, this is fairly primitive propaganda but worth posting for historical context.

Is it fake? Is it real
When Propaganda Lines Are Blurred

All hell broke loose on the Internet in May of 2016 when people thought Hillary Clinton's media team released a new ad called, "Are You Man Enough". In fact, nobody could tell if it was fake or real.

Figure 18: I'm Man Enough to Vote for Hillary Clinton
Real or Fake? You Decide.

Figure 19: I'm Man Enough to Vote for Hillary Clinton

Regrettably for the Hillary camp, the model that was used in the ad was also used for Syphilis awareness in Portland, OR.

.

Lines Blurred

Why would people not know if an ad is real or not? Well, any good propaganda effort may have 100's or even 1000's of social media flockers working in tandem. However, as one of the laws of Modern Propaganda states: *Revealing the truth undermines the message.* What this means is that in the digital world you lose credibility when social media followers realize you are just part of a team developed to sway minds. Furthermore, as this meme shows, if one of your campaigns go wrong you can simply say it's fake, if it goes well, you can simply show it as sign of support from the public.

Figure 20: Return of Pajama Boy. I'm Not Man Enough.

Once the "I'm Man Enough" ad went viral it did not take long for the "Pajama Boy" to resurface.

Figure 21: I'm Man Enough

Trying to further add to the credibility of a potential fake ad, models started to pop up around the Internet giving the ad a very professional look and feel. This was a classic blurring of the lines move by Clinton's opponents or an incredibly stupid attempt by her propaganda team to make the ads look good. In Modern Propaganda grey is good.

Figure 22: I'm Not With Her

After the viral storm created by the "Man Enough" ads, Clinton opponents attack on gender equity, making the point you should vote for the most qualified candidate. Many suspect this ad was put out by the Sander's Propaganda Team.

Figure 23: I'm Man Enough

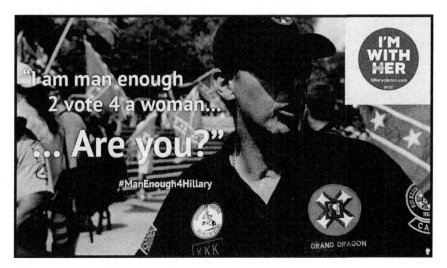

No Modern Propaganda effort would be complete without accusing the opponent of racism, as shown by, this KKK meme.

Viners, YouTubers, and Streamers Oh My: The Next Generation
Traditional TV and Cable are in the process of a full scale technological
disruption. However, unlike the music industry that simply ignored the
likes of Napster and tried to legally force the old reality of non-digital
music on consumers, TV executives seem to have learned the lesson.
They understand that the eyes have moved from the large screen of the
TV to the small screens of IPhones. However, while traditional
entertainment seems to have found a path forward on the Internet, the
most impactful disruption is coming organically from the next
generation of Viners, YouTubers, and Streamers. This group, among all
others who fall within the realm of celebrity, will have the greatest
influence on Modern Propaganda.

Vine Comedian - Thomas Sanders
Sander's, famous for his Story Time Vine wrote, "It always takes me
aback that the videos I make can positively affect someone somewhere
in the world." Aside from being one of the most well-known of the
Viners this generation has produced, he clearly understands he can help
others with his fame. Using comedy, he's leveraged his fame to do
good.

Figure 24: A Collection of Thomas Sanders' Vines and YouTube

The Egg Surprise Lady

Thought to be amongst the highest paid YouTube earners with estimates ranging from $3 to nearly $5 million, The Egg Surprise Lady Brazilian-born Daiane DeJesus, is a product marketers dream. Her influence on children is well known as they seem to gravitate towards her childlike talking and sounds.

Figure 25: The Egg Surprise Lady Influencing Children

The Epic Meal Bacon Guys

Eat big or go home. These guys are a blessing to the food industry without even trying. They tap into the health conscious counter culture of America that targets guys, beer and bacon, oh yea, and epic meals. With an audience reach that far exceeds most TV food shows, The Epic Meal Guys are becoming a massive disruption to traditional TV food advertising. Hey, if you can't beat 'em, join 'em.

Figure 26: Epic Meal Guys

Figure 27: Marques Brownlee also known by his stage name MKBHD

With over 3 million subscribers Marques has been Influencing the world of Tech Gadgets since 2009. His well-spoken manner and demonstrations of the latest's and greatest allows him to influence buyers. If you're trying to reach the tech consumer product market segment, his influence could help you on your way.

Figure 28: Michelle Phan is an American make-up demonstrator

With over 8 million subscribers, Michelle Phan is a Vietnamese-American make-up artist and owner of skincare line IQQU; she produces beauty tutorial videos and is the spokesperson for Lancôme.

When it comes to Modern Propaganda, the question comes down to this simple thought: Is it better to use a well-known celebrity for your TV ads or does an Internet star have more direct influence? As the shift from TV to Internet slowly takes hold, this will be the most debated marketing question of our time.

I could go into exhaustive detail as there are 1000's of more digital influences with more arising every day that you could harvest for your campaigns. For your convenience, I have included a list in the Appendix from Wikipedia, called **YouTubers and Viners According to Wikipedia,** which I hope you will find of use.

8
ACTIONABLE INTELLIGENCE & PAY TO PLAY INFLUENCE

Turning Big Data into Action

Everything you hear today involves the words, "big data". The catchphrase has become so systemic that enterprises and organizations are enamored with the mere mention of it. But why? What is all the hub-bub about? The answer is twofold. Number 1: Organizations now have the ability to collect vast sums of user data. Number 2: The marketing director of large organizations think big data is cool.

Unfortunately, this leaves the tech staff sitting on a goldmine of actionable information that is difficult to distill to the rest of the organization because of the *"curse of knowledge"*.

> ***The "curse of knowledge" is a cognitive bias that leads better-informed parties to find it extremely difficult to assess problems from the perspective of lesser-informed parties.***

This can be represented by the simple equation:
*$P*Ck^2=D$ (Power*Curse of Knowledge^2=Disaster)*

Therefore, all the data in the world will do you no good with solving your main issue which is controlling the direction of the masses and individuals. You must create a system in your organization that delivers actionable intelligence to the parties that need it. How would you go about doing this? Well, you need not fret. Fortunately, Modern Propaganda relies heavily on actionable data models.

Simplicity Is Key

Converting actionable intelligence starts with simplifying the message you are trying to convey in order to get the action you wish to achieve. For example, if we wanted a group of people to walk on the left side of the road, we may selectively release data that shows that most deaths occur on the right side of road. Or, in the case of an Internet website, we may show, by using heat mapping data tools, that the majority of users click on the upper right hand corner of a website. Therefore, that becomes a website's most valuable real estate and so on.

Data is a very powerful tool in Modern Propaganda as it allows you to selectively distribute information to get an end result you wish to achieve. Without controlling and understanding the data you will have very little opportunity to achieve your end goals. A lack of understanding leaves the door open for challenge and mistrust.

While technically classified as Data Science, one does not need be a scientist to be a data scientist. One must simply have the proper acumen and be willing to put in the time to read the data reports, which will be abundant. Over time, and with practice, you will be able to pick the data you want to disseminate, and like a modern day alchemist, be able to convert seemingly useless data into actionable gold.

It's About the Data, Stupid

Over the next 100 years, I fully expect predictive data analytics to drive Modern Propaganda. As data is harvested from individuals, you and your team will use this to predict and drive user behavior. There will come a point in time where you will be driving past a billboard on the road and your smart car will transmit a signal that will change the board to something you might like to see. Or in the case of predictive analytics, a software program will take the average of all the drivers to show a billboard ad of what most people would like to see.

Many people will think this type of smart content is creepy. However, as with all things, eventually the population will come to accept and enjoy the new reality of personalized propaganda.

While the thought of a personalized billboard based on your smart car's data is exciting there is a way to go. Fortunately, plenty of technology is available now that you can use to your strategic, digital advantage.

Thoughts on the Curse of Knowledge and Internet Consulting
It should be noted that some of the most untrustworthy businesses that will try to hire and harm consultants are spammers or jumpers. Jumpers are businesses that will continuously hire multiple vendors to do their digital media work. They constantly seek the next big thing in tech, all while thinking they know better. They are like drug addicts in that they need the fix, yet, they are despicable in nature, constantly seeking to harm and sue you. Meanwhile, their websites are infected with pharmacies, pornography and gambling related items. Even presented with the reality of the amount of work you had to do to fix their problem, they will soon threaten you and seek your demise.

The Curse of Success
When it comes to Modern Propaganda, the bigger and better the job you have done the more you must appease. That is to say, when you work with a large client in the digital world and achieve a measure of success, you must appease them to continue to do so. The issue is that the client, and more importantly, the client's employees will quickly realize that they lacked the digital knowledge and expertise to be successful. Your success creates a situation where the employee feels threated as it may cost them their job. Furthermore, the business will begin to feel like they could be put into a hostage situation where their success is dependent upon you.

Success is both a blessing and a curse, and many times more of a curse. We have countless examples and case studies where ad agencies and digital consultants worldwide have demonstrated this phenomenon. The issue comes down to the variability and fragility of the human ego. Ego will lead an otherwise competent employee to undermine and seek to devalue your work so they may get ahead.

To navigate these waters, you must seek to appease the client's ego, without appeasement. You must also appease the client without damaging or allowing them to damage the success you have created. These two goals can be difficult to achieve, therefore, you must use cunning and deception to help the client win.

Success to Theft

Did you ever wonder why so many software providers have backdoors, server validation and other provisions to shut you down in case you don't pay? This is because in the early days when many digital experts achieved success their work was stolen and reused. In the age of digital marketing, we face a similar issue, and the situation is not as simplistic as placing a server validation key into software. This is because, as well as what was mentioned above, success drives theft and creates a false sense of illusion to the client.

To the client, when success is achieved, all but the most seasoned CEO's immediately believe they can simply take over the success you have created without understanding the work or what went into creating it. They will hire staff, replicate and move you aside. Or worse, they will put their faith in another consultant or hire a marketing manager who sees plunder for the taking. While these clever creatures are neither technologically sophisticated nor competent, they do talk with a silver tongue. They will gladly capitalize and plunder the success you have created all while driving you out.

Unless you are able to stop this process it will start a spiral which will result in you slowly being moved out of the organization. Here is where it gets interesting. While it's easy to look at success as simple once it's achieved, it is also easy to take success for granted. It's easy to overlook the countless hours of labor, the lessons, the drive and sheer grit success requires. Therefore, as you leave it soon erodes, at which time they will blame you for their failure.

Sad? Yes. Annoying? Yes. Should you retaliate? No. Provided the account has paid and fulfilled all of its obligations you must simply walk away. Well, not exactly. You must walk away and find a new client in the same market space and build them up, to not only compete, but destroy your newly formed competitor.

Success is all that matters.

9
MOBILE PHONES, IT'S A PERSONAL THING
HOW TO HARVEST A VENGEFUL INTERNET

We indoctrinate our children to believe in the lies and manufactured reality around us. Then, one day, they wake up and realize that the world around them is built on paid media and consumerism. What Apple understood before many high tech companies is: *people want to hold, control, and dominate the products they own*. They embrace them and love them as if the object is a part of their identity and being. Many people cannot stand the thought of someone else touching their phone, let alone using it or scrolling through the photos or apps located within its digital environment.

It is not a mere phone;
it's a personal extension of self.

This is not instinctive behavior. It is trained and can be cultured in almost every human being on earth. With this training, phones are now considered identity or persona and, therefore, become very fertile ground for Modern Propaganda.

Mobile Me
Mobile devices dominate our world by tapping into mass distribution of information. However, it is difficult to penetrate these distribution channels with paying. 1The best way to tap into this power is to purchase advertising on Google and Facebook. The key to this method is to feed into the emotional state of your target group with ads. Fear

and anger, as well as, tapping into the need of people to do good deeds, can be an effective position to take while buying ads.

Many professional marketers are familiar with tapping into this emotional state and refer to these states as "Vitamins" or "Painkillers". In simple terms, a Vitamin is a very common message or product and a Painkiller is a must have message or product. If you consider the sizes of most mobile devices on the market you quickly realize your message must be compelling and effective or you risk wasting valuable resources on buying unneeded ads.

I am of the opinion that regardless of how common a product may be, if one crafts the message in such a way that it is backed by data, the common man will buy it in groves.

Harvesting Vengeance – Going from Mobile to Nuclear
Have you ever heard the term, "Going Nuclear"?

Well, in the old days of the Internet, this meant attacks on an Internet presence or website using a denial of service attack. While still potent on the global stage, denial of service attacks are outdated tech. Now, this is not to say by any means that such an attack is no longer potent and can still cause a painful disruption to your online competitor. However, government and large organizations can effectively shut down these attacks. This was demonstrated by the U.S. government as it essentially blocked North Korean access to the Internet. China, also, will from time to time, stop communication in segments of its society by blocking data access.

Therefore, today's digital army must rely on propaganda distribution rather than brute force. What do I mean by this? Well, it is true that there are master independent hackers who can take down whole systems to make a point. However, it is more likely that the best hackers either work in the private sector or for a government agency. On one hand, the private sector hacker would not risk going to jail. And on the other hand, the public sector hacker is already in alignment with the power structures that allow for little independence.

Infiltrating the mobile Internet with propaganda is not as simple as it sounds. As I mentioned previously, it is simpler to buy mobile paid media if your message is not one that will be blocked by the places you wish to advertise.

However, when ads are not an option and your cause is one that requires discretion, you will need to take a few basic steps. In addition to some of the tactics I have already mentioned in earlier parts of the book, you will need to learn deception, infiltration and encryption.

Deception

There are many ways to deceive and some people are more comfortable doing this than others. The goal is to distribute and control propaganda. Therefore, your command center will partially be from your mobile device which you must mask.

Using hidden app tools, or vaults, is one way to accomplish this for the task. Fundamentally, the best tools hide behind a legitimate app, storing photos or data behind a locked door. More sophisticated data vault apps can go into a stealth mode of sorts where the app will only show as an icon on your phone screen when you enter a secret code, or sequence of taps. They will also alert you of break-in attempts and some will even wipe your phone clean in case it's stolen.

Some of my favorite tools include: Gallery Lock Lite, Keep Safe, Vaulty, and KYMS which disguises the app as a calculator.

Jailbreaking

This an essential skill for deception. Jailbreaking is a way to modify your phone in a manner that unlocks restrictions placed upon it by the creators. Using a tool like Pangu when you jailbreak a phone allows you to access Root, or as the older Linux service admins would call it, *God Mode*.

The reason companies like Apple and Google place restrictions on devices is to, not only protect the consumer from mistakenly installing dangerous apps that can destroy their phone, but to control the business environment in which they operate. For example, Apple might wish to limit your use of an IPhone to only AT&T.

The secondary effect of jailbreaking a device is that it allows governments to place date tracking and backdoors onto the mobile device, making it more effective for law enforcement and military to do their job. This assumes that said government has not already made a deal with Apple or Google to collect data as needed, which is unlikely. Additional reasons to jailbreak a phone would be to install special encryption software that is not approved by the Apple store or local government.

I prefer to keep and use older devices, since they often don't have the latest technology that may prevent jailbreaking.

10
GLOBAL INFORMATION, GLOBAL SPIN

> *How you wield power and more importantly how the public interprets the power you are wielding is critical.*

To illustrate the above statement, I would like to look back at the presidency of George W. Bush. His presidency started rather mundane, until the events of September 11, 2001 occurred, which propelled him and America into the world spotlight as we initiated global military action to combat a threat that the United States had let simmer for years prior. In taking the military action, many political opponents were able to seize upon and plant the political seeds of decent due to an over reaching of military force by the administration and a war weary public with little tolerance for the realities and bloodshed.

By the time the next election came about, the cooperating media outlets, planted protest groups and paid activists were able to stir the public into such a frenzy of despair that they were all but begging for help. This gave his political opponents the chance to capitalize and take power. However, this was not remarkable.

The remarkable portion came once President Obama was elected to power. His political team managed to all but stop the war protests, calm the public into obedience to the government, wield the media to create a "USA is good again" message to the rest of the world and even receive a Nobel peace prize. All this was achieved while continuing the wars, yet calling them criminal actions, not closing Guantanamo Bay, and even engaging in targeted killing of U.S. citizens. This was further compounded by the military use of drone strikes to kill combatants which were not only more lethal than the techniques used at Guantanamo Bay, Cuba but killed women and children.

One would think mass war protests would start all over again once these events were reported in the news. This assumption would be false. Not only were there no protests, but the masses actually embraced the "war no war" state as a new beginning, a new hope.

This comes back to a simple and singular point. Were the masses or the war protesters sincere or even real? Were they truly wanting to stop the wars? If so, where are all these protesters now? Where were they when that jet bombed a hospital? Where are they now? The answer is: Yes, the protests were real. It's just that the protesters did not realize they were being manipulated as part of a larger power struggle.

This is the true power of Modern Propaganda.
It is about using your ability as a leader
to strategically move the masses to achieve your goals.

It is about understanding that while unsavory, the masses want you to lie to them, and never want to be exposed to the full detail and truth. The masses like their beef packaged nicely, as to not see the slaughter. From war to business, from public to client, what you will encounter will be the same. They like to believe they have control, while giving control to you.

The age of Modern Propaganda has only begun. As technology progresses to connect everything we know, it will only be a matter of time before every aspect of people's lives can be controlled and leveraged. You will be controlled or you will be a controller in the end.

> **It is better to build your own reality than to have one built for you.**

Do I believe any U.S. President or political organization would intentionally inflict harm upon a society? Absolutely not. However, in the digital age where disruption is the norm, they may not be able to comprehend the changing world around them and, therefore, may become puppets, not leaders.

Modern Warfare and Armies in the Digital Age

Modern warfare is one of the most difficult ideas for the mass population to grasp. Driven by a digital viral models armies are no longer state actors. Instead the Internet and its decentralized communication network of apps, games, and encrypted underground has allowed and facilitated armies formed without the need of state. These armies are decentralized and can be formed with significantly less resources than were required by the armies of old. Combined with the use of Modern Propaganda, this has become a powerful force to be reckoned with. As in the past, some armies can adapt to new techniques of warfare and some cannot.

I am torn on the subject; in one aspect the masses are their own worst enemy. Driven by what is referred to as political correctness they fail to see or acknowledge they are even in a war. They cannot grasp how one or two individuals can with proper resource and intelligence can build an army of global proportions. Therefore, it is not an army in the minds of the masses. This allows the attacking army to slaughter the ignorant citizenship.

The effect is that while they are culled, they will instead focus on gaining political points for their respective party. That being said there is benefit to this slumber. Instead of setting the masses in a panic they continue to consume keeping the economy flowing, all while being in a state of war.

Thoughts on Warfare Propaganda
Along the same lines of thinking of how modern warfare and armies have evolved so too has warfare propaganda. While modern decentralized armies have mastered Modern Propaganda through the use of social media so too have enemy media outlets. I suspect that some media organizations have been created and funded by foreign entities for the purpose of Modern Propaganda. By this, I mean they use propaganda as a media smoke screen allowing them to deny or justify the existence of modern armies which makes it easier for decentralized armies to attack. While in countries like the U.S., where free speech is a central pillar, such organizations have come to be expected in society and are tolerated. Even in countries where this is not the case we must consider the following.

While this business of warfare is unseemly, the simplicity of the model is both elegant and lethal and should be looked at if one is doing propaganda or planning attacks on an enemy state or territory. This model may be more difficult to achieve where "media" is state controlled but in a society where free speech is tolerated this has proven to be effective.

Arm a Population When You Trust It, Disarm Them When You Do Not
In the United States, the Right to Bear Arms was put in place by the country's founding fathers as a way to ensure individuals could always defend themselves from enemies, both foreign and domestic. Ever wonder why gun control advocates, and in more extreme cases, gun removal advocates never seem to reach their goal despite many horrific incidences involving guns? The answer is surprisingly simple and something the founders of the United States understood. In fact, it has been understood since the times of Rome. Those who bear arms are typically willing to put their lives on the line to defend their rights, those who wish to control the rights of others to bear arms are willing to put the lives of **others at risk,** yet, not their own to accomplish the goal.

Notes about Leadership
You must have victory. Those not driven with enough passion to win and do their jobs will contribute to your demise. Lethargy and lack of action is a death nail in the digital world. Far worse are leaders who lack vision or drive to understand the digital world. You must not only keep up with the digital industry you must constantly leap frog it to win.

11
A PATH NOT FOLLOWED

Many of us hold the belief that the Internet and technology gives each person a very individual experience; a chance to express themselves like never before, a chance to watch and listen to any type of entertainment they choose, a chance to sort through the propaganda of old and carve a new path for future generations. In the beginning this was true and to some extent still can be.

However, as 2014 approached, it was clear to all but the most ardent government supporter we had failed. Instead of more freedom, every aspect of life was recorded and monitored. Instead of independent journalism every story was used to sway opinion for political gain.

It was also clear to those of us in the technology/media area that the press had willingly given up its 4th amendment rights. Instead of a willingness to challenge government officials on facts of legislation, it promoted it as part of a political party.

Some Internet firms, like Reddit, took strong, decisive action blocking what they coined *advocacy journalism.* However, from the Iraq war to health care, lie after lie was fed to the American people and they loved it.

War Not War
America has been in a constant state of war since 9/11/2001. Many propagandists attempt to label this warfare as *criminal action*, thereby extending the state of war and the war footing the country has been on, by making war more palatable to the masses. I only write this to showcase and demonstrate that the strategy of calling ***war*** a ***criminal***

action has been completely effective and an example to learn from when discussing propaganda strategy.

This single change in perception management of moving *warfare* to *criminal action* accomplished two goals:

1. It stopped mass protests in America and across the globe by putting the population into a needed submissive state. Tamping these protests down was critical, as the population was beginning to force actual structural change to government and society. Once the population was submissive again, it allowed for the continuation of the warfare without the noise of the mob.
2. It allowed the government to convey benefits to the masses, making them more dependent upon the state they once despised. If the masses had not been placed into a submissive state, they would have rejected the benefits as suspicious and sought self-sufficient means to exist. To this extent, I say it is acceptable to have some in society thrive and break the bonds of dependency upon the state, but not for all. For how can one have a government if there is no one to rule? This fine balance must be maintained. People must be dependent to make government relevant.

The Pendulum Effect
The zig-zag and dance of societal control is called *the pendulum effect*. In fact, in Modern Propaganda it is so powerful you could literally take a country to war and have no protests, yet, under a different leader you could have massive protests.

There are many factors involved, but today's generation is particularly susceptible to the pendulum effect created by party politics and war couched in social liberalism. This method of control tamps down your traditional protesters while allowing a government to carry on with its intended activities with very little opposition.

The pendulum effect also allows for the passage of laws designed to makes people's lives "better". On the surface, the laws look attractive. However, as the full impact of these laws come to bear, millions of Americans are waking up, and the harsh reality is that the definition of "better" to a government bureaucrat is not necessarily what is better for the individual.

Many times the legislative aides who write the laws are so greatly disconnected from an individual citizen's actual wishes that they write the laws simply based on which lobbyist has paid them the most. Thus, resulting in a loss of freedom. Furthermore, the constant state of war has ensured that every man, woman and child is being spied on, thus, eliminating another layer of the Constitution and freedom.

For the first time ever, a U.S. citizen has defected to Russia, no longer able to stand the clear violations of the Constitution. However, there was nothing more than a peep in the media.

It should be known that while writing this book, I seriously question America's ability to turn the corner back towards freedom and liberty. Every law passed seems to be sold to the highest bidder.

However, from the perspective of Modern Propaganda, it is not our job to worry about the masses except to the extent that we need to sway them. We must simply understand how to control them and practice what has been shown effective in delivering the desired result

Is this cynical? Perhaps. Is this ethical? That is unknown.

What I do know is the world around us has been created by individuals. The rules you assume are absolute are nothing more than ideas and concepts created by others.

> *It is your prerogative to*
> *EITHER be ruled or to be the ruler*
> *of your world and the reality around you.*

Modern Propaganda is shaping where humanity is heading, those who can wield it will change the future, those who cannot will simply accept "what is" as life.

12
PEACEFUL PROTEST, DIGITAL VIOLENCE
THE PROPER USE OF VIOLENCE

> *Those who seek violence will often get violence,*
> *those who seek hate will often get hate.*

This is true of real life and the digital world but blending digital violence with real world violence to control your message can be difficult and dangerous, if not done correctly. To be very clear, I am not advocating violence as it can result in harm to the innocent and lead to uncontrolled situations with unspeakable horror. Furthermore, violent action may quickly sway opinion against you. Nonetheless it is used as a control mechanism in countless countries and as part of the political process in many western countries such as the United States.

Violence, when used correctly, has been shown to silence political views, create a sense of outrage, and unify opposition. Even in countries like the United States, where the right to free speech is built into The Constitution, many individuals and power brokers still believe and advocate for the stifling of speech with the use of violence. Even here, in a Westernized society, it is has been shown to be effective.

In the situations of dictatorships and other countries without free speech, rights differ. For example, in Westernized nations, a leader cannot simply slaughter or starve the population into submission. In Westernized nations one must have two factors at play to use violence:

1. The target must be despised by a portion of the population.
2. The media must be swayed to agree with this opinion.

Provided these two factors are achieved, a limited amount of violence will be tolerated and can be highly effective in achieving your goal of suppressing dissenting or unsavory opinions that are unfavorable to your cause.

While the assessment upon the target individual is certainly subject to one's opinion, and hate speech is technically what is protected by the Constitution, it matters not. Using Modern Propaganda methods, one can begin priming the pump in the mind of the masses to give an opponent the image of the despicable. This is a critical first step if one plans on using violence to silence one's opponent which I will review in the next section.

You Disgust Me
Once the image of disdain is painted upon a target, you only need to feign innocence to use violence to silence the wagging tongue of the enemy.

To illustrate, I give you the example of the Presidential candidate, Donald Trump. While the rise of his popularity first seemed absurd to some and despicable to others, he hit a tone with a segment of the masses that was unexpected to those in opposition, likely to him, and more importantly his opponent's propaganda teams. They, like many, missed the boat to attack him early and hard. This is a common mistake when one underestimates one's enemy.

> *Allow others to do violence on your behalf*
> *and distance yourself from the mob.*

This error in judgment by the opponent's propaganda team was corrected when Trump was effectively silenced at his own political rally in Chicago, IL. By using violence as a last resort, they were able to steer the propaganda narrative for mass consumption. This was necessary because Trump's opponents had lost control of the narrative, media and more importantly power.

Ultimately, you never want to get to this point, but if you need to use violence just make sure it's the proper use of violence.

The Proper Use of Violence
Taking the Trump example as *the proper use of violence*, it is prudent for us to examine how this was achieved.

First is what I call the feeling phase. This is where the propaganda team must carefully explore the data surrounding an opponent and *feel* where the violence threshold is. This is because violence has a threshold of socially acceptable norms. There is always a certain amount of violence a society will tolerate, provided it results in a perceived gain.

Like musicians, the violence threshold of a society is more of an intuitive feeling than a calibrated absolute. This feeling makes it difficult for some to judge correctly. However, a seasoned professional will know exactly where the populace stands.

In the case of Trump, the first step was to begin the grooming of the public with intense social media swarms (See Chapter 3), combined with Hate meme images of Trump (Chapter 7), and layering of charges of bigotry. Many of these tactics I have covered in previous chapters so I will not digress.

Of the three tactics used, the grooming with the hate memes provided the most effective solution. Further opportunity came when the opponent's media team captured Trump's audience, or a plant, using a pledge that looked similar to the salute that was used by Hitler.

This image allowed the team to create a massive amount of viral hate meme images that sewed the narrative of Trump being racist, and even worse, as evil as Hitler. As expected, these spread like wild fire and were gladly consumed by reporters and individuals alike. This was a rather trivial undertaking as Trump has demonized and insulted large segments of the population, thereby contributing to efforts against him.

Next was the distillation of a broad and simplistic marketing message of Bigotry, Evil, Hate (BEH). The BEH message was applied and constantly reinforced through social media to ensure the grooming would take hold. This, too, was fairly easy to achieve association because the target, Donald Trump, tended to use language that is considered politically incorrect.

Keep in mind, none of this would be possible if followers did not want to be lied to. Obviously, Trump is not Hitler. However, the wish by many that he is Hitler allows the mind to justify stopping his free speech rights. The grooming of the public perception even extended into spelling bees where viewers reported instances of personalities from local radio stations in Northampton, MA joking with audience members about how horrible Trump, and Republicans in general, were. These same stations also claim to cover political news in a non-biased manner. While instances of reporters were not directly correlated to the propaganda efforts, it centrally helps the cause by influencing the grass roots population.

Once the priming of the minds took place in social media, and the seeds were planted in the reporter's minds, the stage was set for "encouraged protests" to take place at a Trump rally Chicago. Some of these "protesters" were actually paid, some were bussed in, others simply arrived as part of a true dislike for the candidate. Regardless, the stage was set for acceptable violence. As the day of the Chicago rally arrived it was clear to many observers that the two groups would be destined to clash, yet either way, Trump would be the loser. On the one hand, if he held his rally, violence would certainly erupt and he would be blamed regardless of who started the violent action. And on the other hand, even if it was clear he did not start the violence, the stage had been set in the mind of the masses that he *deserved* it or *caused* it.

This sets the stage for *the proper use of violence*.

Blocking Roadways, Preventing Gatherings
You have tried everything! Viral lies, Social Media Swarms, and you even have members of the press in your back pocket.   Nothing is working and your opponent is gathering more and more followers and somehow, some way, creating a message that resonates with the masses.

This leaves a few options and blame will not help.

With that in mind, we know at some point most leaders will want to make actual contact with real people. We also know, no speech can take place if followers cannot get to a physical place to gather. Yes, the Internet is ideal for viral communication, and yes, much of the information we wish to communicate to our followers can be accomplished over the web, yet, at some point a leader and its followers must gather.

Therefore, action must take place to prevent the momentum from continuing. You must influence your followers to protest and block roadways that provide the transportation route to events of your target. Doing so has the benefit of getting news media attention, stopping your competitor's message, and showing your cause is just and righteous.

Many think that the "road blocking protests" are spontaneous. This is a false assumption. While there are indeed some spontaneous blockings, the vast majority are built up by advanced Modern Propaganda efforts which guide the suspecting and unsuspecting to action. Furthermore, the wise propagandist will know how to read and understand when this is happening to them, as well as, know when to do the same to someone else.

As for the legalities of such actions, they are questionable and depending on the country you reside in, I will leave that to your discretion.

Yin and Yang

Many may ask how a provocateur and reality celebrity such as Trump can rise to such a status. The opponents call him and his followers vial, racist, and uneducated. To that extent, this is where the phenomena lies. I submit to you, this simple, psychological profile of the rise of Trump. Whereas the political elite, who have greater experience than I, may differ; I see this as a simple yin and yang scenario.

This is a deep rooted issue of a lot of the Trump supporters who grew up and were educated in middle class schools and were "rough around the edges" types of Americans. The Trump opposition were more gentile in nature and perhaps did not fit into the norms of school. As a young person, this has a profound effect upon one's perception of the rest of society. This roughness gave the Trump type supporters an advantage during the high school years.

> **Guide the flowing waters of perception to your advantage.**

As time often does, this advantage became a disadvantage as the ones who did not fit in soon became the artists, professors and well educated populace. This also moved the role of being *the one provoked* to being *the provocateur* and *judge* of how the populace should behave in a society they have the advantage in. For a few generations, this new role had the effective means of transforming society and norms. However, it also had the bully effect because while it was true many of the middle class needed more culturing and acceptance of others, many were simply hard working people who were being stereotyped and grouped as racists, sexist and bigots like the ones who did not fit in during their younger years.

This, then, moves those who would not normally support a type like Trump to lash out upon those who attack them. Thus, the cycle of yin and yang continues. Regardless of what political persuasion you may hold, as a propagandist you must learn to guide the flowing water of perception to your advantage.

Caught
The Digital Violence Threshold
Violence is acceptable when used in the context of an evil opponent. However, what happens when the peaceful, open-minded protesters turn on their own party? Here too, the digital world plays a critical role. Although, in this case, the role of digital is that of losing control of the mob. This is due to the fact that while it may be acceptable to use violence under the guise of peaceful protests against an opponent, it is not acceptable to use this same tact against one's own party.

Let us look at the example of Bernie Sanders and Hillary Clinton. When Bernie's supporters were blocking roads and inciting violent actions against Trump's all too willing supporters, it was easy to blame Trump, for he was *the enemy* and *the enemy* is evil by nature. Many on Twitter, Facebook and other Internet media outlets were all too willing to look the other way. This changed when Bernie's supporters realized the same tactics that were being used against the opponent were being used against the Sander's camp as well. This was further compounded by the inherent dilemma that many of the Sander's supporters were protesters during the George W. Bush years and were against war and Wall Street funding of candidates. Sanders supporters not only realized the fact that Hillary Clinton received heavy funding from Wall Street corporations but, by necessity of her position in government, participated in numerous actions that involved war and the military.

The peaceful, violent protesters were confronted with a moral dilemma: ignore the truth that they were part of a lie just to win an election, or hold what was true to them and turn on Clinton. While most simply sulked back to accept the forthcoming victory of Clinton, the true hard core did not, and propelled by social media rage, projected the violence against Hillary. This leads us to a lesson.

> ## Never expose your followers to the truth.

For, if that façade breaks, the wise propagandist must quickly act to quell the mob you created. You, as the propagandist, must also accept responsibility for the violence you have provoked on the untrained minds. Once you allow the truth to be exposed, you must act quickly on social media to demonstrate how evil the enemy is and that by turning on your own party you will help the enemy. If that does not work, you must resort to shaming and calling out the violence you created. There will be a select few that will question why the violence is now wrong when it was accepted against the enemy, but that will be the few.

Getting Graphic
Whereas the Trump example is an effective form of combining digital propaganda with real world violence, this pales in comparison to the use of violent, digital propaganda from the group ISIS. Nonetheless, as despicable as the group has become worldwide, we must look at their use of propaganda as it has achieved a limited amount of success.

The real key was recruiting Westerners who were savvy in Modern Propaganda. They understood that showcasing extreme violence such as live beheadings, burning people alive in cages, and slaughtering of innocent children would get media attention. Furthermore, instead of indiscriminately killing, they would stage the killing as if on a movie set. This was to make it palatable to Western tastes, groomed by years of Hollywood violence, and to give it a viral effect on social media.

> *While not as widely used, Hollywood movies can be an effective cornerstone of any Modern Propaganda campaign.*

While filming the violent scenes, the group even went to the extent of telling the victims they would not be killed simply to get the proper camera angle. The result was Western media loved it, viral social groups spread it, and people wept over it. Ultimately, this gave the group a means to broadcast a message to a worldwide audience of billions.

Loathsome as these propaganda tactics are they can work. However, if you cross the violence threshold you will be destroyed by it.

Where Does it All lead?
As with all great shifts and disruptions in society, the age of Modern Propaganda is one such phase of an ever evolving continuum, the Information Age.

And, like our forefathers who labored to lay railways across the vastness of the globe to ignite the Industrial Revolution, workers of the Information Age labored laying a global fiber optic web of light and copper to businesses and households across the globe. This web of networked complexity further extended to wireless points and smart devices that touched all aspects of human existence. Yet, this backbone does not, unto itself, make the internet or the Information Age as it is just a foundation. For, without information, data, and the software to move the internet, it is nothing but roads upon which nobody drives.

The age of Modern Propaganda is simply a logical continuum of this foundation. It is not just about basic talking points and spin, but the control and influence of whole societies. To do so, countries, leaders, marketers and modern web architects must understand how to wield the information that flows across these vast networks. This is not about controlling societies with blunt force but controlling societies and individuals to behave by design.

Every line, every word, every thought scripted for consumption and driven by data.

Those who emerge as masters of the art of Modern Propaganda will be the leaders and influencers of tomorrow.

...And one more thing, as with all things, there are rule and laws that govern a system, including Modern Propaganda. With that, I empower you with **The 26 Laws of Modern Propaganda**.

The 26 Laws of Modern Propaganda

Laws of Modern Propaganda - Law 1
A person would rather hear a lie than hear the truth.

Laws of Modern Propaganda - Law 2
It is acceptable to lie to a person who understands they are being lied to; if it facilitates their goals, they will simply look the other way.

Laws of Modern Propaganda - Law 3
If you lie, you will have a strategic advantage temporarily, however, this advantage will erode over time because results are needed to sustain a lie.

Laws of Modern Propaganda - Law 4
Always take the high road, except when the low road is required.

Laws of Modern Propaganda - Law 5
Propaganda exists when corruption is real.

Laws of Modern Propaganda - Law 6
Never let a tragic event go unexploited or your enemies go unaffected.

Laws of Modern Propaganda - Law 7
Always use double speak to confuse an enemy.
"Soldiers and cops are murderous thugs. Only soldiers and cops should have guns."   This tactic will result in outrage AND love from the common. It will leave those who think logically, and therefore pose a real threat to your propaganda efforts, in a twisted in a loop.

Laws of Modern Propaganda - Law 8
Manipulation is an art, not a science.
It is best to manipulate people in social media through words, 2nd best through memes and viral video, 3rd best through manipulated search engines, 4th best through journalists, and 5th best through celebrities. This is because celebrities are costly, journalists are fickle, search is subject to algorithmic updates, viral memes and video are fads, and social groups retain lasting anger and seek revenge.

Laws of Modern Propaganda - Law 9
Bigotry is your friend.
Calling someone racist, sexist, or otherwise bigoted is the fastest way to win followers on the Internet. On one hand, it looks like you are defending a good cause; on the other hand, those who are against the enemy do not care if it's true. Either way you gain followers.

Laws of Modern Propaganda - Law 10
Fake users get you started, real uses keep you going.
For every 1,000 fake users, you can gain influence with 100 real users. However, this effect will erode as the deception becomes obvious, so know when to quit.

Laws of Modern Propaganda - Law 11
Enrage, engage, be disdained.
You must always establish social media accounts which enrage users and accounts that delight users. This way you can play both sides.

Laws of Modern Propaganda - Law 12
Rewards are for the few, not for the many.
Always encourage elitism. People are naturally awed by power and celebrity. By doing so you can preach activism without having to follow the restrictions. This allows you to maintain your resources while looking virtuous to your followers.

Laws of Modern Propaganda - Law 13
Journalists are activists who seek to be exploited.
Most journalists are lazy and biased. Therefore, you should submit press releases when news sources are less abundant and feed them biased stories they will greedily digest. This will save them the work of having to find a news story and feed their activist intentions.

Laws of Modern Propaganda - Law 14
Raise your enemies stature to undermine their message.
Blaming all your ill's upon an enemy is a sure way to get praise whether you caused them or not.

Laws of Modern Propaganda - Law 15
Assume the media is corrupt for it is.
Simply beat the drums of war and the media will follow. It need not be an actual war, it may simply be a political enemy or foe. Once you create a "drum beat moment" your cause is almost unstoppable.

Laws of Modern Propaganda - Law 16
Data is difficult to defend, yet, easy to manipulate.
When you don't have technical prowess, create data analytics that cast the business and competitor in a negative light. When you possess technical prowess point out the competitor's technical flaws directly. On the one hand the technical flaws are difficult to dispute for they are facts, and in the case of data analytics they can be difficult to defend for they are amorphous.

Laws of Modern Propaganda - Law 17
Hate them like you love them.
The best form of baiting a user on social media is hate reading, 2nd best is sex, 3rd best is number lists, and 4th best is cuteness. Cuteness makes you feel good, number lists make your mind work, sex is intense but limits the reach, while hate cuts across all spectrums.

Laws of Modern Propaganda - Law 18
Burn Bright and Fast
You have 0.5 seconds to engage a user, 3 seconds to enrage a user, and 5 seconds to delight a user. I say: delight them when you can, enrage them if you need to, and engage them when you have time.

Laws of Modern Propaganda - Law 19
To turn a user into a follower is easy; to turn them into a disciple is difficult.

Therefore, I say you must get a user to invest at least 3 minutes of time; 3 minutes of time will get a commitment, 4 minutes of time will get an interest, and 5 minutes of time will get them to prophesize. Whether through dispute or agreement it matters not. However, any more than 5 minutes of time will eat into their patience, any less than 3 minutes of time will eat into their commitment.

Laws of Modern Propaganda - Law 20
The more complex the data, the more simplistic you must present it. The more simplistic the data, the more complex you must present it.

In the case of simplistic data, the user will assume they can do the task on their own, therefore, present it as complex so they won't even try. In the case of complex data, present it in a simplistic manner so that the user will quickly realize, through deduction, that it is complex and leave you to your task.

Laws of Modern Propaganda - Law 21
It's not lying, if you don't say anything.

When communicating digital information, if you tell an unpleasant truth before earning trust, a person will disdain you. Therefore, it is best to avoid disclosing information too soon. By earning their trust first, they will listen and embrace you when you tell them the truth.

Laws of Modern Propaganda - Law 22
A client with *perceived* technical experience will always blame you for their ills.

The client will blame you if a technical clean-up is necessary and despise you if you succeed in cleaning up their technical issues, as you inadvertently pointed out their flaws. Either way they will leave you and you will waste time.

Laws of Modern Propaganda - Law 23
Break ones trust to allow the propaganda to flow.

Once you are able to break the trust of a government or organization, through their own accord or yours, the masses will readily accept propaganda.

Laws of Modern Propaganda - Law 24
Call it what it's not.

When bribing legislators, never use the word "bribe", instead use the words "lobbying" or "donation". This way you keep the public's mind at ease and avoid the legal ramifications of using truthful language.

Laws of Modern Propaganda - Law 25
Your intent is never nefarious; it is always for the good of the individual.

Laws of Modern Propaganda - Law 26
It's the law. It must be true.

J.M. del Hagen

Appendix
Useful Notes & Random Thoughts

Thoughts on Manufactured Reality
Today's population seeks manufactured reality. Starting with the most fundamental of things. Products are delivered to them in the form of packaged meats, processed chicken, artificially colored foods, GMO's, fast food, and on and on.

This need also drives the public's insatiable appetite for reality TV, which is, in fact, manufactured reality. The public uses reality TV to escape their own reality, by viewing someone who is dysfunctional, that they can criticize. The reality TV also allows them to participate in a drama they might not otherwise get.

Thoughts On "The Pendulum Effect"
As I noted earlier the phenomenon I call "The Pendulum Effect" is where a government maintains power and accomplishes its goals through the use of a two party political system propaganda. In the digital age, I say this is still one of the most effective forms of social control possible and allows one to control a population with the least evil. Therefore, if you are able to establish such a system it is best to do so. Brutality, force and coercion will only get you so far and while they attract certain individuals, especially when paired with social media, it is an untenable state of control that will eventually collapse.

Thoughts on Promoting a Single Story as News
While distributing a single news story across multiple media outlets was a mainstay of the past, the same methodology does, indeed, seem to hold true in the age of Modern Propaganda. This is driven in part by a lethargic attitude of reporters, combined with a lack of resources to generate original news, but not alone. The news reporters also prefer a single news story so they can discuss their views with peers. This confluence makes it a particularly attractive target for those looking to wield influence over the masses.

Thoughts on Media Bias

MSNBC, originally owned by GE, on the surface seems to have been created as an offset to Fox News. However, it's primarily a Liberal news outlet used to further corporate agendas. From a propaganda point of view, the channel is ideally leveraged for stirring up protests or tamping them down if you're a social Liberal or Democrat. It has also been effectively used to drive massive pieces of legislation to the benefit of huge multinational corporations. While the station's ratings are normally on the low side it made our Modern Propaganda list for its ability to have Democratic party news fed to and ingested by the station.

Fox News

This darling of the Conservative and Republican Party was the first news outlet to cover Conservative topics giving it unprecedented growth in a time where other cable outlets were declining.

Very Conservative leaning with a patriotic slant Fox news can be used to drive the topics that are Conservative in nature. Primarily used by Republicans the channel also has a strong base of Libertarians which are socially liberal but fiscally conservative when it comes to government. You have to be a bit careful when feeding Fox News the news. Unlike a news channel like MSNBC that claims to be Progressive, but will support the Democratic Party regardless of actions, Fox News has been known to turn on the Republican Party if Conservative values are not followed.

CBS News

This is one of the original network news outlets long before cable arrived. My opinion is they do their best to maintain a traditional news value.

Huffington Post

Democratic Party not Progressive. The Huffington post is basically an extension of the Democratic Party. Recent examples include the Democratic President Barack Obama war in Syria. In most cases the Progressive wing of the Democratic Party would protest war over dictators killing their own people, in the case where it's a democratic president that needs to go to war you can be sure the Post can be used to blame republicans this creating a distraction to the true progressive while the war escalates.

Blame and misdirection is the game here.

Washington Post
Fairly neutral, with a slightly right of center slant. However, it seems to follow the political climate in Washington DC.

CNN - Slight left of the political spectrum.

ABC Political - Yahoo
This online outlet is manufactured political news with a DNC view. I suspect many political news stories here are in fact press releases from the DNC

NBC - Network news with a classical left slant.

Talk Radio - Mostly hard right coverage and entertainment.

Thoughts on Targetable Media Outlets
The following are the top 100 newspapers with digital footprints. Work with them and exploit them for your own gain.

1. Wall Street Journal
2. USA Today
3. New York Times
4. Los Angeles Times
5. San Jose Mercury News
6. New York Post
7. Washington Post
8. New York Daily News
9. Chicago Sun-Times
10. Chicago Tribune
11. Dallas Morning News
12. Denver Post
13. Newsday
14. Houston Chronicle
15. Philadelphia Inquirer
16. Arizona Republic

17. Minneapolis Star Tribune
18. Tampa Bay Times
19. Orange County Register
20. Newark Star-Ledger
21. Portland Oregonian
22. Cleveland Plain Dealer
23. Seattle Times
24. Detroit Free Press
25. U-T San Diego
26. San Francisco Chronicle
27. Boston Globe
28. Las Vegas Review-Journal
29. St. Paul Pioneer Press
30. Kansas City Star
31. Sacramento Bee
32. Fort Worth Star-Telegram
33. Pittsburgh Post-Gazette
34. Pittsburgh Tribune-Review
35. St. Louis Post-Dispatch
36. Milwaukee Journal Sentinel
37. Baltimore Sun
38. Arkansas Democrat-Gazette
39. Atlanta Journal-Constitution
40. Orlando Sentinel
41. Indianapolis Star
42. Miami Herald
43. Louisville Courier-Journal
44. South Florida Sun-Sentinel
45. Buffalo News
46. Bergen County Record
47. Charlotte Observer
48. Tampa Tribune
49. Cincinnati Enquirer
50. Virginian-Pilot
51. San Antonio Express-News
52. Columbus Dispatch
53. Omaha World-Herald
54. New Orleans Times-Picayune
55. Hartford Courant
56. Riverside Press-Enterprise

57. Oklahoman
58. Raleigh News & Observer
59. Austin American-Statesman
60. Honolulu Star-Advertiser
61. Memphis Commercial Appeal
62. Nashville Tennessean
63. Rochester Democrat and Chronicle
64. Providence Journal
65. Detroit News
66. Salt Lake Tribune
67. Palm Beach Post
68. Philadelphia Daily News
69. Richmond Times-Dispatch
70. Boston Herald
71. Fresno Bee
72. Birmingham News
73. Des Moines Register
74. Allentown Morning Call
75. Arlington Heights Daily Herald
76. Florida Times-Union
77. Asbury Park Press
78. Tulsa World
79. Arizona Daily Star
80. La Opinion
81. Toledo Blade
82. Los Angeles Daily News
83. Washington Times
84. Dayton Daily News
85. Lexington Herald-Leader
86. Akron Beacon Journal
87. Charleston Post and Courier
88. Northwest Indiana Times
89. Albuquerque Journal
90. Vero Beach Press Journal
91. Deseret News
92. Delaware News Journal
93. Wisconsin State Journal (WSJ)
94. Long Beach Press-Telegram
95. Mobile Press-Register
96. Knoxville News Sentinel

97. Roanoke Times
98. Syracuse Post-Standard
99. Tacoma News Tribune
100. Baton Rouge Advocate
101. Torrance Daily Breeze
102. Chattanooga Times Free Press
103. U-T North County Times
104. Worcester Telegram & Gazette
105. White Plains Journal News
106. South Carolina State
107. El Paso Times
108. Harrisburg Patriot-News
109. Colorado Springs Gazette
110. Spokane Spokesman-Review
111. Grand Rapids Press
112. Daytona Beach News-Journal

Thoughts on 3rd Party Candidates

In fact, both political parties participate in the *pendulum effect* by ensuring that no 3rd party candidates have an opportunity to be elected to political office. They do this by passing laws that sway the advantage towards the two party system. States pass laws that prevent an Independent candidate from raising equal amounts of campaign funding as either the Republican or Democratic challengers. While unfair, this type of manual intervention is critical in keeping the two party system in control of the political process.

The same is true for spying on one's own population. While many times these activities are set in the name of security, it is easier to violate the Constitution when done by a leader who is socially Liberal. The public perception is that the social Liberal leader has not broken the Constitutional law enough to warrant further protest or scrutiny, while a Conservative leader will not be afforded the same luxury. Given that each party has broken the law equally, justice is therefore swayed by controlling public perception and leveraging the media.

Thoughts On Gaming
"Gaming for Gold"
Ever hear of Slither.io? How about Agar.io? No? Maybe? Well, I can assure you the youth of today has and many savory propagandists are taking advantage of this fact. Simply by labeling your character with your cause will help you reach 1000's. Yes, it's tacky but who cares.

Thoughts on Propaganda Teams
The Team
I am not going to spend a lot of time describing how to build an organization designed to distribute propaganda. For one, it is extremely difficult identifying qualified individuals without making an in person assessment of an individual, and two this is not a business management book.

What I will tell you is that in today's world, the individual knowledge worker makes up the factory line of old. Each person has a specific set of unique and overlapping skills to create the line.

Personality wise, these people do not want to be just an *'employee'* and while money is important for many, it is not the deciding factor in their working equation.

That being said, in building out a knowledge based team I have a particular recipe of individuals which I find works best. The basic organization structure can be scaled depending on the size of the needs. For example, if the team was needed for modern information warfare against an enemy state you would perhaps want to scale to 100x or even 1000x times the size. However, for a basic political or brand campaign you may not need to scale at all.

HR Me Not
Let's discuss a bit of the non-politically correct realities of a team. To start, y*our team must at all times be kept in information bubbles while conveying a sense of transparency and common vision.* This means, while the Architect and Creative Director may have a full view into the complete objectives, it is unwise to allow the Writers, Programmers and other team members to ever fully understand the entire picture. This keeps the team slightly off balance, leaving an air of mystery to the organization. This mystery can feel seductive and give a sense of

importance. Furthermore, this reduces any moral objections the team may have to the work if, or when, it becomes unseemly; which can happen when working with propaganda.

In particular, Engineers and Coders have higher perceived ethical standards and may turn on you quickly. Allow your Architect to control these resources directly and eliminate them if needed. Coders have a tendency to refuse to do work even if you're paying them, and if they do the work you can be sure it has been done with spite and possible destruction. I have witnessed many ignorant Human Resource people who may be accustomed to running a traditional post century office attempt to lead a knowledge based organization, resulting in chaos and halting productivity. In a knowledge or creativity based organization, Human Resources is just that, a resource.

Avoid allowing Operations Managers to hire knowledge staff. These individuals may be talented in process, however, they often lack the technical depth needed to understand the content and larger mission. When they make hiring decisions they tend to choose knowledge workers or coders *they understand and can control*, not those who are qualified. This is an important point to keep in mind. They hire workers they *"Understand"* and '*Can Control*" not those who are qualified. At all costs you want to avoid the bloating of unqualified personnel and mutiny from the qualified engineering staff.

Quickly Eliminate the Weak and Lazy
Whenever possible weed out staff as soon as practical. Allowing unqualified or disruptive knowledge workers to continue because they are liked will simply result in long-term, unpredictable damage. The most drastic damage tends to come from those with access to the source code of the organization. I have worked with teams where coders have been '*working*' only to find out that the seemingly simple functions they wrote surfaced as bugs during updates months later. Allowing unqualified engineers or knowledge workers to operate for even short timeframes can result in technological debt that extends far past the term of the worker. The unqualified manager will lack the understanding of how to identify these individuals and may fight for them to stay on staff.

The "Qualified" Unqualified

The technology industry is full of individuals who can convincingly lead an organization to its destruction. Everyone is a "tech person" or has some magical formulation. The vast majority of these "tech visionaries" are incompetent at best and liars at worst. However, they can be convincing to even seasoned professionals.

I decided early on that I would not be writing a management book. However, the part of building a knowledge based workforce is so critical that if you get it wrong you may doom yourself. So I give you this limited final advice on team building: The Architect / entrepreneur business type is critical to lead your organization to success. They are not only executors and driven but fully understand the content and details through an intimate understanding of the product or goals. They have marketing, technical ability, and business leadership skills. Without this you will create a team that mimics and copies others in the industry instead of leads. This will result in the demise of your organization since the Internet is fluid and rapidly changing. Yesterday's business models are already outdated.

1. **The Architect**

   Unless you're an expert in Internet technology architecture, this is perhaps your most critical hire. These are the guys and gals that many jokes have been written about where a clever cartoon shows a black hat mirrored by a white hat. The joke is that everything they build is *gray*. It is difficult to distill this profile onto paper as it can look overwhelming and random to the average HR person. A mistake in hiring here can cost you the entire organization and become a threat to the survival of the team. Therefore, I recommend this hire be done the in the same manner you would hire an executive level position.
   Compatibility: Digital Strategist, Business Development, CEO

2. **Creative Director**

   Creative or Crazy, maybe a little of both. Again, this is more of an executive level hire with lots of freedom given to the individual you hire. This person is an expert in visual messaging and strategic positioning. The Creative Director and the Architect are binary stars that work hand in hand. He or she should be highly energetic and able to tap into the emotional

elements required to reach the ever diverse consumer.
Compatibility: Digital Strategist, Business Development, CEO

3. **Executors**

   Executors are in some ways the nemesis, as well as, the internal drivers of the organization. They help execute the mission. While their drive and detail orientated nature is critical, it can also lead others astray. The executors tend to want to do every task even if they are not the most qualified. They may also limit the development of the organization if not in their proper role.
   Compatibility: Accountant, Operations Manager

4. **Software Developers**

   I have found that, to work effectively, you need three software developers in a unit. Preferably they will have a strong background in what is called the LAMP stack and be very familiar with the world of open source. Each will have slightly overlapping skill sets.

   A. The primary will be near expert level in server side build out, scripting and deployment with the ability to code more difficult problems using regular expressions. Typical skills include: Perl, PHP, Apache, MySQL & Java.

   B. The secondary is what I call the "Bulldozer". They will be able to drive the project forward and be your executioner. This person is critical for getting the job done since many engineers classically over promise and underestimate the scale and scope of a project. He or she is your driver. Typical skills include: PHP, MySQL, CSS, HTML 5, jQuery, JavaScript.

   C. Thirdly is your Front End Coder. This person is detail oriented and typically used for putting together the visual elements that the target audience sees. They will help you get the proper CSS formats in order and skin the websites or digital media you wish to distribute. Typical skills include: HTML5, CSS & Schema.org data setups. **Compatibility:** Project Manager

5. **Graphic Designers**
   I have found in my years, there are two types of designers: production level designers and creative visionaries. The Architect will need both skill sets in order to create a productive propaganda system. **Compatibility:** Creative Copywriter

6. **Copy and Content Writers**
   A critical tier of the team are two senior writers. Typically, the former newspaper reporters are well suited as they are a very familiar with the news cycles and media and tend to be excellent investigative resources. The most difficult part will be training them in your particular area of need. However, I have found that the newspaper reporting opportunities are limited, and not very well paying, so they tend to be eager to master your vertical market. The two senior writers will take the roles of editor and workflow writing manager respectively. It should be noted that the personality trait of these writers tends to be a bit calmer and less aggressive by nature which is ideal for reporting and writing but less ideal for project management. Therefore, one must consider another a project manager to oversee the writing staff. **Compatibility:** Public Relations, Reporters

7. **Social Media Writer**
   This person makes catchy headlines, is great at quick witted arguments on Twitter & Facebook and can instinctively community build. Use them to inflame or delight your social media user base. **Compatibility:** Social Media Coordinator

8. **Data Analyst**
   This person, along with the Architect, helps read the proverbial tea leaves. Typical skill sets will include: data analysis of analytics, webmaster and social media report tools, viral and global trends, tracking search terms, producing reports and graphs. **Compatibility:** Digital Strategist

9. **Content Manager**
   This person is responsible for loading and tagging digital content in everything from your website to your Facebook pages. **Compatibility:** Subordinate

10. **Content Producer**

    Unlike the writers, this person can produce and create viral videos, glitch gifs & Jpegs, and other interesting media that will be used to grab a consumer's attention. **Compatibility:** Graphic Artist

11. **Social Media Coordinator**

    Manages the automated tools that post to social media accounts. **Compatibility:** Subordinate

12. **Public Relations**

    I find you typically need two well spoken, attractive female or male spokespeople to answer questions and attend events. These are the face of your organization. **Compatibility:** Copywriter, Business Development

13. **Business Development**

    This individual will help facilitate any 3rd party data or advertising deals that may be needed to penetrate a particular market segment. Sometimes paying is the path of least resistance. **Compatibility:** Public Relations

The Puppet Master

Only a fool would leave an Architect to his own will. While, it is true your architecture is your most valuable asset, it is also true that they can be your worst enemy. Therefore, the Puppet Master is responsible for not only mustering the financial resources to fund the propaganda team, but also the leveraging of financial resources as a control mechanism. The power of the purse gives you the ability to question and observe. Take care with the Architect and make all efforts not to be a foil, instead you're a counterbalance. **Compatibility:** CEO

Appendix 1: A Citations

1 Page 28, *Men risk their lives to save burning man in Clifton Park,*
Timesunion.com:
http://www.timesunion.com/local/article/Men-risk-their-lives-to-save-
a-burning-man-5679028.php

2 Page 29, *Adam Myers `14 Risks Life in Heroic Rescue Attempt*
Siena Saints website:
http://www.sienasaints.com/sports/m-soccer/spec-rel/081114aac.html

3 Pages 30-32, *Guilt by Wikipedia: How Joe Streater Became Falsely
Attached to the Boston College Point Shaving Scandal,*
Awfulannouncing.com:
http://awfulannouncing.com/2014/guilt-wikipedia-joe-streater-
became-falsely-attached-boston-college-point-shaving-scandal.html

4 Page 40, *Sued by Google, a State Attorney General Retreats, New York
Times website*

Nytimes.com:
http://www.nytimes.com/2014/12/20/technology/google-attorney-
general-jim-hood-lawsuit.html?_r=0

5 Page 40, *Google Sues to Block Mississippi Attorney General's Probe,
Alleging Ties to MPAA, Variety.com*
http://variety.com/2014/digital/news/google-countersues-mississippi-
attorney-general-alleging-ties-to-mpaa-1201383637/

6, 7 Page 40-41, *Google vs. MPAA Showdown: 5 Fast Facts You Need to
Know, By Stephanie Dube Dwilson at Heavy.com*
http://heavy.com/news/2015/08/google-sues-attorney-general-jim-
hood-mpaa-lawsuit-sopa/

8 Page 42, nytimes.com article
http://www.nytimes.com/aponline/2015/04/11/business/ap-us-google-
mississippi-attorney-general.html **NO LONGER AVAILABLE**

9 Page 44 The Verge
http://www.theverge.com/2015/3/9/8164357/apple-watch-event-700-

<u>million-iphones-sold</u>

10, 11 Page 52, Wikipedia: Campaign for "santorum" neologism
<u>https://en.wikipedia.org/wiki/Campaign_for_%22santorum%22_neologism</u>

12 Page 56 *Amazon sues alleged reviews-for-pay sites, cnet.com*
http://www.cnet.com/news/amazon-sues-alleged-reviews-for-pay-sites/

Helpful Data Chart in Order Of Magnitude (Wikipedia)

Decimal		
1000	kB	kilobyte
1000^2	MB	megabyte
1000^3	GB	gigabyte
1000^4	TB	terabyte
1000^5	PB	petabyte
1000^6	EB	exabyte
1000^7	ZB	zettabyte

ABOUT THE AUTHOR

J.M. del Hagen is a recipient of the esteemed Robinson Hall award for Global Information Architecture and Propaganda. Considered the leading intellectual and founder of Modern Propaganda, he has won countless awards for his Internet systems architecture and use of data science to drive consumer, brand marketing. He is recognized worldwide as a pioneer in the use of Artificial Intelligence to drive human political influence.

Printed in Great Britain
by Amazon

39166570R00079